Three Dishes One Soup

Inside the Singapore Kitchen

Lace Zhang

Marshall Cavendish Cuisine

Editor: Lydia Leong
Designer: Bernard Go Kwang Meng
All photographs by Lace Zhang except those on
pages 6, 8, 10, 14, 16, 17, 47, 106 and 108 by Teresa Teng

Reprinted 2019, 2020

Published by Marshall Cavendish Cuisine
An imprint of Marshall Cavendish International

A member of the Times Publishing Group

Other Marshall Cavendish Offices:
Marshall Cavendish Corporation, 800 Westchester Ave, Suite N-641, Rye Brook, NY 10573, USA ▪ Marshall Cavendish International (Thailand) Co Ltd, 253 Asoke, 16th Flr, Sukhumvit 21 Road, Klongtoey Nua, Wattana, Bangkok 10110, Thailand ▪ Marshall Cavendish (Malaysia) Sdn Bhd, Times Subang, Lot 46, Subang Hi-Tech Industrial Park, Batu Tiga, 40000 Shah Alam, Selangor Darul Ehsan, Malaysia

National Library Board, Singapore Cataloguing-in-Publication Data

Names: Zhang, Lace.
Title: Three dishes one soup : inside the Singapore kitchen / Lace Zhang.
Description: Singapore : Marshall Cavendish Cuisine, [2018]
Identifiers: OCN 1017762089 | 978-981-47-9456-5 (paperback)
Subjects: LCSH: Cooking, Singaporean. | Cooking, Chinese. | LCGFT: Cookbooks.
Classification: DDC 641.595957--dc23

Printed in Singapore

To my mummy and daddy

Contents

Acknowledgements

This book would not have been possible without:

My granny, who feeds the family so well and takes care of us so selflessly. She sparked the initial concept of this book and she is the glue that binds everyone together. We are truly spoilt by her.

Auntie Alicia, who took care of me when I was younger and helped cook all our Lunar New Year meals. She patiently taught me how to make all these familiar dishes. It wouldn't be the same without her food.

My mummy and daddy, who helped me get all the ingredients for doing this book while I was busy at work. They taste-tested what I cooked and gave me feedback about the food. My dad finally revealed his secret of being an excellent cook and shared all the amazing dishes he watched my grandpa make.

Ian, for all his valuable advice.

Steph, from Anywhere Social, who helped with the website (www.aroundthediningtable.com) and for her genuine involvement and interest in this little project of mine.

Yaoen and Guofeng, who helped take the photo that would eventually become the cover page!

Carol and Teresa, who helped with the very first mock-up of the book. It has now evolved into a completely different animal, but some pictures used here are the ones taken by Teresa for the initial draft.

Violet and Auntie Eileen, who generously loaned me the cutlery for the first mock-up of this book.

Lennard and Tiffanie, who contributed their recipes, and Kimberly, who gave me the idea of making chicken essence from stories of her mum.

Lydia, my editor, for taking the chance to meet with a girl who had a dream to write a cookbook and ultimately to make all this possible... She helped fine-tune things, gave me advice and encouraged me to take the pictures for this book all on my own — something I would never have attempted otherwise — allowing me to learn so much more in the process.

> Food is Memories.
>
> ~ The Hundred-Foot Journey

Introduction

I look around the wooden table, every inch laden with a dish or a pot. There's golden and gleaming *ngoh hiong*, piping hot and crisply promising; there's sweet and sour fish, glistening red and interspersed with chunks of pineapple; there's a plate of stir-fried vegetables, two kinds of roast meats chopped into chunks, stir-fried noodles for the vegetarians, pork belly stewed in soy sauce with whole unpeeled garlic cloves nestled between chunks of tender meat, a plate of fried chicken wings, braised bean curd skin and a pot of collagen-rich fish maw soup, chock-full of ingredients...

I am amazed at how my maternal grandmother always manages to whip up this spectacular feast all on her own every Lunar New Year. Her tiny living room is filled with members of my extended family, a rare occurrence that we are all gathered together, sharing glimpses of our lives and filling up on granny's food. I spy my grandma, her diminutive frame at the kitchen door and her eyes slightly watery... she mutters "*wo hen gao xin ni men duo lai le.*" (It makes me so happy to see all of you here.) This is why she cooks.

Frankly, this book was borne in part due to fear. Fear that these treasured recipes will be lost along the way, and with it, a part of our culture. Fear that one day, there would be no one to prepare all these familiar dishes we grew up eating, that there would be one less reason for everyone to come together. Hence, I started to learn to cook next to my grandma, documenting her recipes with precise measurements as opposed to "*agak-agak*" (estimating the quantities), much to her chagrin. "There's no need to weigh, just anyhow," she would say whenever she saw me whipping out the kitchen scale. Cooking is instinctive to her. She has spent most of her life cooking, day in and day out, a pinch of this, a splash of that — everything comes naturally to her. And by some form of alchemy, her cooking is always consistent and her food always tastes the same. She measures, not with a scale, but with her expert's mind, based on years of experience. She adds calculated dashes of seasoning and gauges the proportion of ingredients used. Cooking has become second nature to her.

Given that many of us do not grow up cooking next to our mothers anymore, nor do we cook daily for our families, I wanted to document the insights and observations I've gleamed from watching someone experienced cook. That being said, although these recipes have been carefully measured, tested and recorded, there will always be many uncontrollable elements in the experiment of cooking. Treat this as a guide to base your cooking on. Revel in the in-the-moment cooking process that everything can and will be different; learn to trust your instincts and make executive decisions to adjust the dish to meet your taste preferences, needs and ideals. This is, after all, part of the excitement of cooking.

Food is not mere sustenance. It is our memories, our history. It is understanding where we come from and it forms a huge part of our identity. Food is a universal language and sometimes, tasting and understanding the food of a foreign culture is almost like being allowed a sneak peak, an insider's pass if you will, straight into their world. Like all things worthwhile, it takes effort to continue the traditions that have long been sustained by previous generations, as we become ever more reliant on the conveniences of the modern world.

The title of this book, *Three Dishes One Soup*, refers to the Chinese custom of having meals, where plain rice is eaten with a few dishes, a good mix of protein and vegetables, all washed down with a clear soup. This way of eating has been ingrained in us as being a complete, nourishing meal, what we would ideally consume for dinner at home, if we're lucky. You can choose to serve just one or two dishes alongside rice, instead of the full works — it's really up to you. Options for one-pot dishes can also be found in the Lunch Staples section if that suits your schedule better.

With my notes and cooking tips consolidated here, I hope to, in my own small way, help preserve a part of our heritage before it is lost in the vestiges of time. This is a book that I hope will help demystify certain aspects of traditional home cooking here in Singapore. It has been many years in the making as it contains recipes of many of the dishes I grew up eating and learned from my maternal grandma, my paternal grandpa and Auntie Alicia, who cooked most of my meals when I was younger. This is a book made up of much of my heart and soul. I hope it finds a way into your life and the lives of your loved ones as well.

Pantry Basics

This section highlights the essentials needed to stock a home pantry. These are the basic condiments and ingredients used in most of my family's dishes, and as long as I've got them in my store cupboard, I feel strangely secure and comforted knowing that a quick meal can be rustled up easily.

CONDIMENTS AND SEASONING

These condiments are essential in the Chinese pantry. They are needed to bring out the distinctive flavours typically associated with Chinese cooking. The supermarket shelves are stacked full of various brands of condiments, and if you are ever in doubt as to which to choose, a general guideline for me would be: the fewer the ingredients and additives listed on the ingredients list, the better the quality.

Light Soy Sauce

Light soy sauce flavours many of our dishes by imparting a savouriness that is deeper and more complex than merely using salt. Quality light soy sauce is made by fermenting soy beans for months and even years to develop its flavour. This results in an amber-hued liquid, enriched with amino acids, contributing to the coveted taste sensation known as umami.

Dark Soy Sauce

Dark soy sauce is made in the same way as light soy sauce but with the addition of molasses or caramel. The resulting sauce is less salty, sweet and thicker in consistency compared to light soy sauce. It is used to add an appealing colour to dishes as well as a tinge of sweetness.

Oyster Sauce

This thick brown sauce adds a savoury flavour to dishes while helping to thicken up sauces that it has been added to. Vegetarian versions are available, made using mushrooms in lieu of oysters. There are also variations made using abalone.

Sesame Oil

This aromatic oil derived from sesame seeds is commonly used to add fragrance to marinades and dishes. It is typically drizzled over dishes towards the end of cooking to retain its fragrance.

Ground White Pepper

In recipes requiring pepper in this book, it is ground white pepper that is used unless otherwise specified. In my family, ground white pepper is the indispensable condiment for adding a dash of snuggly warmth to any dish.

Salt

Where salt is used in these recipes, I have used fine sea salt. Should you be using coarser flakes of salt or fine table salt, do taste and make the necessary adjustments.

DRIED GOODS

The Chinese have been using dried goods in their cooking for centuries. This ancient method of preservation helped stretch the shelf life of foods long before the refrigerator was invented. The drying process reduces the water content of the food, concentrating and intensifying its flavours. What was borne out of necessity has changed the culinary landscape. It's amazing how a little really goes a long way in helping to amp up flavours in a dish.

Dried Shrimps

Also known as *hae bee* in Hokkien, *ha mai* in Cantonese or *xia mi* in Mandarin, these tiny, dried shrimps are indispensable in Chinese cooking. A handful will add a punch to stir-fried vegetables or noodles. It can also be used to bulk up certain dishes like glutinous rice or yam rice. It is almost magical how these add so much flavour to dishes. Soak the dried shrimps in water for 10–15 minutes to rehydrate before using. Don't soak them for too long or the flavour will leach into the liquid. Store dried shrimps in an airtight container in a cool, dry place or in the refrigerator.

Dried Scallops

Sometimes also known as conpoy, dried scallops vary in price depending on their quality, origin and size. The most expensive ones hail from Japan. Dried scallops are commonly used to sweeten and intensify the flavour of soups, stews and sauces. Soak in water for about 30 minutes to rehydrate before using. The soaking liquid can be reserved for use in the dish. Store dried scallops in an airtight container in a cool, dry place or in the refrigerator.

Dried Chinese Mushrooms

These mushrooms have an intense flavour. When used in braises, stews and stir-fries, they act as sponges and will soak up the flavour of the dish. To prepare, soak them in hot or warm water for 15–20 minutes until softened. Trim the tough stems and discard. The soft, fleshy caps can be sliced or used whole. The meaty texture of dried Chinese mushrooms makes them perfect for bulking up vegetarian dishes.

Chinese Sausages

Known as *lup cheong* in Cantonese, these Chinese sausages are made from cured minced pork. They usually come speckled with bits of fat, which is also what makes them taste so good. They add a tinge of savoury richness and sweetness to dishes.

White Peppercorns
Oyster Sauce
Sesame Oil
Light Soy Sauce
Dark Soy Sauce

Dried Chinese Mushrooms
Dried Shrimps
Dried Scallops
Chinese Sausages

Pantry Essentials

Rice and Rice Porridge

Rice is a staple of our diet here and my preference is for Thai fragrant rice (also known as Thai *hom mali* or jasmine rice). Growing up, I would watch my auntie rinse the rice, then use her fingers to measure the ratio of water to rice in the rice cooker. To do this, place the tip of your index finger on the surface of the rice in the pot, then add enough water to reach the first joint on your finger. Alternatively, I find that 1 part rice to $1^1/_4$ parts water works like a charm. Close the lid, turn on the rice cooker and let it cook. Fluff the rice with a spatula or with chopsticks before serving. If you don't have a rice cooker, you could either invest in a small, cheap and cheery one, or cook the rice in a covered saucepan over extremely low heat until the water has evaporated. Turn off the heat and leave the rice to sit undisturbed for 10 minutes before removing the lid and fluffing the rice.

For rice porridge, here's a rough guide that would serve about four with regular appetites. Rinse 200 g long grain rice and place in a pot with 900 ml water. Peel a medium size sweet potato and cut it into small chunks. Boil for about 20 minutes or until the sweet potato is tender. This recipe yields a slightly watery porridge where the rice grains are still visible. I find this bland, soupy porridge incredibly soothing, with the sweet potato chunks adding a touch of sweetness and textural contrast. Any leftovers can be used to make porridge *kueh* (page 92) for another marvellous meal.

Fried Shallots/Garlic and Shallot/Garlic Oil
These are precious, bronzed aromatics that can add an oomph of flavour and crunch to anything. They flavour noodle soups and provide a punch to fried rice or dried, saucy noodles. You can also toss them in salads for crunch in lieu of croutons. Store them in clean, dry airtight containers in a cool, dark place. They should keep well for 3–4 weeks.

To prepare fried shallots, peel, then slice the shallots thinly and pat-dry with paper towels. In a wok over medium-low heat, heat sufficient oil to cover the shallots. Add the sliced shallots and fry until just lightly golden brown. Remove and drain well. The shallots will continue to brown in the residual heat. Do not leave them in the oil to brown or they will burn. I find it best to cook shallots over medium-low heat as you get better control over the heat and the shallots brown more evenly. Store the fried shallots in a separate jar from the oil.

Fried garlic can be prepared in a similar way, but the garlic should be minced or finely chopped. Be even more careful when frying garlic as they can go from toasty to burnt in a matter of seconds.

Liquid Lard and Lard Croutons
I like to keep a jar of this rendered lard on hand. It can be used in place of cooking oil and lends lends amazing flavour and unctuousness to dishes it is added to. The resulting crispy lard croutons can also be used to top noodles (such as Hokkien prawn mee soup, page 28), or if you're feeling naughty, eaten as a snack, seasoned with a little vinegar and salt or light soy sauce.

Chop about 500 g pork fat into small cubes. Heat a saucepan or wok over medium-low heat and add the pork fat and 2 tablespoons water. Let the fat render until the little cubes of pork fat turn an appetising, golden hue. Drain and set these cubes aside to cool. They will crisp upon cooling.

Store the liquid lard and lard croutons separately in clean dry containers and use as needed. I find the lard croutons go a little rancid and soggy after 2 weeks so I don't keep them for longer than that.

The liquid lard can be used in place of oil for stir-frying. It can also be drizzled into soups or tossed with noodles. It will keep well in the fridge for up to 4 months.

Dried Shrimp Sambal (Hae Bee Hiam)

This is an aromatic, flavourful and quintessential condiment that can be used to jazz up just about any dish. It is fabulous eaten neat from the jar, tossed with noodles (see pantry noodles, page 34) or used as a filling for deep-fried spring rolls. I even add them to cookie dough to make an addictive buttery, spicy-salty-sweet cookie for the Lunar New Year.

Traditionally, recipes for dried shrimp sambal do not include the use of dried scallops, but this recipe below is from my Auntie Alicia who adds them to amp up the luxe quotient. She fries up one mean spice paste! Admittedly, dried shrimp sambal does require significant effort to prepare, but you can make a batch and it will last a pretty long time stored in the fridge, if you exercise sufficient self-restraint!

Ingredients

300 g dried shrimps
100 g dried scallops
200 g shallots, peeled
200 g garlic, peeled
300 g big red chillies
250 g small red chillies
200 ml cooking oil
½ Tbsp rock sugar
½ Tbsp salt

Method

1. Soak the dried shrimps and scallops separately in water for about 20 minutes until softened. Drain well. Pound the dried shrimps and scallops separately using a mortar and pestle or a food processor until fine.
2. In a blender, blend the shallots, garlic and chillies into a fine purée.
3. Place a wok over medium-high heat. Add the oil and swirl it around the wok. Add the pounded dried shrimps and fry until lightly golden brown. Add the pounded dried scallops and repeat to fry until crisp and golden. This will take 8–10 minutes.
4. Add the shallot purée and top the wok up with more oil if the mixture starts looking dry. Continue frying the paste over medium-low heat until the mixture is well caramelised and becomes a deep, burnished red. This could take another 30–45 minutes.
5. Season to taste with rock sugar and salt. Let the mixture cool completely before storing in clean airtight jars in the fridge.

"For is there any practice less selfish,
any labour less alienated, any time less wasted,
than preparing something delicious and
nourishing for the people you love?"

~ Michael Pollan

Lunch Staples

As a kid returning home from the drudgery of school, lunch was always the highlight of my day. I longed to return home to familiar comforts like Auntie Alicia's delicious lunches, cartoon reruns or a game or two of Nintendo, while plopped atop a slouchy beanbag chair with a can of ice cold soft drink within reach, clearly without any parental supervision.

I was fortunate enough (then) to have a helper, Auntie Alicia, a passionate and conscientious cook. She prepared most of my meals growing up, carefully and with heart. Even a simple weekday lunch would be sumptuous under Auntie Alicia's watchful care. Noodles? Stir-fried, in soup or even hand-kneaded. You name it. One of my favourite dishes was a comforting noodle soup with fish balls and slices of fishcake, the calm note of the broth rattled only by a jolt of aromatic fried shallots. Auntie Alicia would regularly spend a good part of the morning slicing, drying and frying those tiny alliums and sealing the crisp bronzed rings in airtight jars. They were the ubiquitous condiment that my family used to spruce up any number of dishes. It provided instant flavour and texture. Another of my favourite dishes was handmade noodles (*mee hoon kueh*), which she made to order.

My maternal grandma would also spoil the family with her fabulous dishes whenever we visited. She would sometimes even deliver lunch boxes to our door, filled with her fried rice, yam and cabbage rice or glutinous rice, always perfectly cooked and seasoned. A common thread amongst most of these dishes is that they are one-pot or one-wok meals, easy on the clean-up and can be left to bubble away on the stovetop as the rest of the household chores get taken care of.

While dinner may seem to be more of a spread with its multitude of dishes and soups, the dishes in this section are truly stand-outs, able to hold their own, titillating and exciting the tastebuds just as well. We may not enjoy them as often now, but when life allows, on leisurely weekends, I like to take a walk down memory lane and revisit some of these dishes, much to the joy of my family.

Century Egg and Minced Meat Congee

Pei Dan Chok

Serves 4–5

Nothing soothes and salves the spirit and body like a bowl of piping hot rice porridge. This is comfort administered on the highest level for the worn and the weary. From the looser, more watery style best enjoyed with salty pickles, to the thicker, heartier congee (featured here), the hallmark of a good bowl of congee or "*juk*", is its smooth mass met with some resistance, not a watery, droopy gloop with the disparate grains of rice still visible. The grains of rice have got to be properly cooked down for it to qualify as proper "*juk*", otherwise, talk to the hand, for you are not real congee!

To amp up the flavour right before serving, add a splash of light soy sauce, a trickle of aromatic sesame oil (or liquid lard, page 16), a spoonful of fried shallots, a small handful of sprightly green coriander or spring onions and a dash of ground white pepper. Even the making of congee provides me with comfort — I find the repetitive, mindless stirring highly therapeutic, watching the coming together of the vast amount of liquid and the tiny amount of rice, resulting in a bowl of something silky, something smooth, something substantial.

2 Tbsp cooking oil
500 g pork bones
120 g long grain rice
45 g white glutinous rice
2 litres water
8 g young ginger
2–3 spring onions
1 tsp salt
½ tsp sugar
80 ml milk
3 century eggs, peeled and chopped

Topping

Chopped spring onions or coriander leaves
Fried shallots (page 16)
Ground white pepper
Sesame oil or light soy sauce

Meatballs

150 g minced pork, preferably with some fat
2½ tsp light soy sauce
A dash of ground white pepper
1 tsp sesame oil
¼ tsp sugar
¼ tsp cornstarch

1. Heat the oil in a wok over medium-high heat. Add the pork bones and sear lightly for a bit of colour.
2. In a big stockpot, add both types of rice, the water, young ginger, spring onions, salt, sugar and the seared pork bones. Let the ingredients simmer over low heat for 1½–2 hours, stirring occasionally to prevent the rice from sticking to the bottom of the pot. The cooking time will depend on how quickly the rice grains break down. At the end of cooking, there should be no visible rice grains and the consistency should be thick. A longer cooking time will yield a thicker congee.
3. Make the meatballs when the congee is cooking. Combine all the ingredients for the meatballs in a bowl and mix using your hands or a pair of chopsticks until the mixture is homogeneous and the colour has lightened. Set aside.
4. When the porridge is done, add the milk and stir. Taste and adjust the seasoning at this point.
5. Form the meatballs into little rounds (using about 1½ tsp mixture per meatball, but don't feel obliged for anything exact) and drop them into the pot of hot congee to cook. Add the century eggs if desired.
6. To serve, ladle the piping hot (and it should be piping hot) congee into warm bowls. Top with sliced spring onions or coriander leaves, fried shallots, a dash of pepper and a drizzle of sesame oil or light soy sauce.

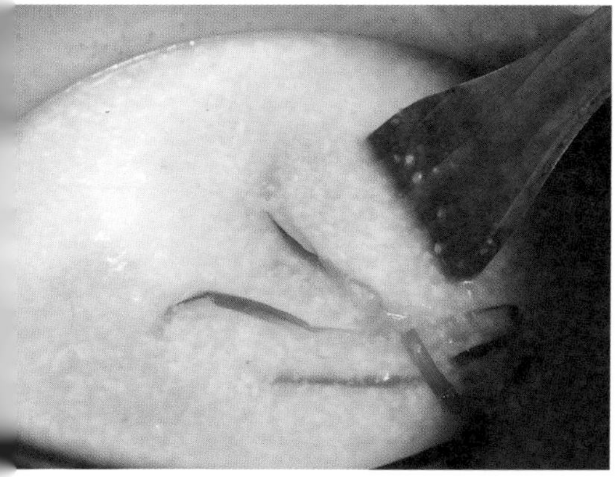

NOTE

- I use a mixture of white long grain rice and glutinous rice when making congee. White glutinous rice, or sticky rice, has an incredibly high level of a starch called amylopectin and using it together with long grain rice will ensure that the congee cooks up to a creamier, stickier consistency.
- What you're looking for ultimately is for both rice and liquid to combine harmoniously and take on a smooth consistency, with no grain of rice visible.
- Adding a splash of milk (any kind you like, even soy milk) towards the end of cooking will result in a creamier, silkier bowl of congee.
- You can also use pork stock in place of water to cook the congee.
- If you are serving this to guests who may be squeamish about eating century eggs, set the eggs aside in a bowl instead of adding them to the congee to cook. Your guests can then help themselves to the eggs.

Fried Rice

Chao Fan

Serves 2 or 1 big eater

Leftover steamed rice. Sizzling garlic. Spring onions. A couple of beaten eggs. All tossed together until the rice is dry, fragrant and dancing around in the wok. There is something very satisfying about using up the odds and ends you have lying around in the kitchen to create a meal. That bit of spring onion stashed in the cooler compartment, the one lone slice of ham in its crumpled paper wrapping or that sad bit of ginger left sitting in the corner. There's no better dish to make use of odds and ends than fried rice.

That being said, I loathe to call this a recipe. It's more a blueprint or an idea. Everyone has their own version of fried rice seared into their food memory bank, the one that grandma or mum cooked so often at home, the one that's familiar and comforting. This is my version of that dish. My grandma always made hers with a good amount of grated ginger, its slight heat permeating the entire dish like a warm hug, and studded with chunks of salty-sweet Chinese sausages and saline chunks of fishcake. This is the style of fried rice I secretly favour and gravitate towards. Food is after all, memory.

1 Chinese sausage (*lup cheong*)
2 eggs
Ground white pepper, as needed
1½ Tbsp neutral-tasting oil such as canola or sunflower oil
1 fishcake, cut into cubes
10 g ginger, peeled and minced
2 cloves garlic, peeled and minced
350 g day-old cooked rice
1 Tbsp light soy sauce
½ tsp fish sauce
1 tsp sesame oil
4–5 spring onions, dark green parts only, sliced

1. Soak the Chinese sausage in water for 5 minutes. Peel off the casing and chop into largish chunks.
2. Beat 2 eggs with ¼ tsp pepper in a small bowl.
3. Heat the oil in a wok over medium heat until it feels relatively hot. Add the Chinese sausage and stir occasionally, allowing the sausage to brown and its flavour to permeate the hot oil.
4. Add the chunks of fishcake and stir-fry for about 1 minute.
5. Add the ginger and garlic, stir-frying until lightly golden brown.
6. Push the ingredients to the side of the wok and pour the beaten eggs into the empty side of the wok. Allow the egg to set three-quarters of the way.
7. Add the rice. Crank up the heat to high and stir-fry everything together like your life depended on it. The goal is to allow the individual ingredients to come together and to toast the rice until some parts are lightly charred. Fry until the rice is golden. This takes about 3 minutes.
8. Add the light soy sauce, fish sauce, sesame oil and ¼ tsp pepper. Continue frying until the seasoning is well distributed. Turn off the heat.
9. Add the spring onions and mix thoroughly. The heat from the rice will release the flavour from within the raw spring onions.
10. Dish out and consume while piping hot! This will warm bellies and souls.

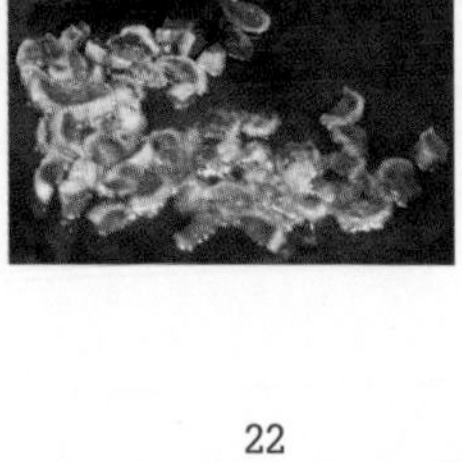

NOTES

- The key to good fried rice is high heat. The rice needs to be cooked sufficiently until the grains are separated and toasty. You know it is done when the rice grains get all riled and heated up, and start jumping around inside the wok.
- Use rice that's completely cool so the grains don't clump together. The perfect rice is day-old rice. Freshly cooked rice contains a lot of moisture and this will prevent the rice from getting that charred, caramelised flavour and colour.
- Old or aged rice will produce fluffier fried rice as the individual grains are drier compared to new crop rice which cook up stickier as it absorbs more water. This is just a point to note, so you'll know why the results may vary.
- I use both fish sauce and light soy sauce as seasoning as they provide different types of savouriness, or umami, to the dish. You can omit the fish sauce and just use light soy sauce as my grandma does.

Yam Rice
Or Png

Serves 3–4

This dish taught me the value of simplicity. As she is Hokkien, my grandma cooks yam rice and cabbage rice — both Hokkien dishes — frequently, and they're splendid versions. When I first tried making this dish, eager to improve on my grandma's recipe, I threw in a whole host of fancy seasonings, thinking it would make the dish more flavourful and look less anaemic, and that I was some sort of a genius. However, the dish came out tasting completely different, with the seasonings overpowering every component of what makes yam rice, yam rice. I learned that the key to this dish is to let the essence of the ingredients shine through naturally, to heighten their flavours with subtlety and not to overwhelm. Fancy strong flavours are not always better.

Here, the yam rice is studded with bronzed dried shrimps, plump and chewy morsels of dried mushrooms, slivers of pork belly and chunks of cubed starchy yam, all nestled amongst savoury rice, their flavours commingling during their sauna session in the rice cooker. I asked my grandma if her own mother's version tasted anything like this. She replied that times were much leaner back then, so the ingredients were not as plentiful. Perhaps, that is why, being the most giving person I know, she feeds everyone so generously with her cooking. To this day, I know of no one else who fills their cooking with as much goodies as my grandma does.

8 dried Chinese mushrooms
50 g dried shrimps
200 g yam
100 g pork belly
Neutral-tasting oil such as canola or sunflower oil, as needed
Salt, as needed
200 g long grain rice, rinsed
½ tsp sugar
1 tsp light soy sauce
A dash of ground white pepper

1. Soak the dried Chinese mushrooms in warm water for about 30 minutes until softened. Squeeze excess water from the soaked mushrooms and measure the soaking liquid. Top it up with more water to make 380 ml. Set this water aside for cooking the rice. Trim and discard the stems of the mushrooms, then cut the caps into large chunks.
2. Soak the dried shrimps in water for about 15 minutes until softened. Drain and set aside.
3. Peel the yam using a vegetable peeler and cut into 2-cm cubes.
4. Cut the pork belly into thin slices across the grain.
5. Place a wok over medium heat and add 2 Tbsp oil. Lower the heat a little and add the dried shrimps. Stir-fry for 5–7 minutes until crisp, fragrant and golden brown. Remove and set aside.
6. Add more oil to the wok if the wok is dry. Heat the oil over medium heat, then add the mushrooms and stir-fry for 2–3 minutes until lightly golden. Season with a pinch of salt.
7. Add the pork belly slices and stir-fry until they gain some colour. Remove the mixture and set aside.
8. Place the rice and 380 ml mushroom soaking liquid into the rice cooker. Add the dried shrimps, mushroom and pork mixture, yam, sugar, light soy sauce and 1 tsp salt. Give it a good stir, then check the water level. You basically want all the ingredients to be just about submerged. Add more water if necessary. Turn on the rice cooker to cook.
9. When done, use chopsticks to give the rice a good stir. Place the lid back on and let the rice sit for another 10 minutes or so before serving.

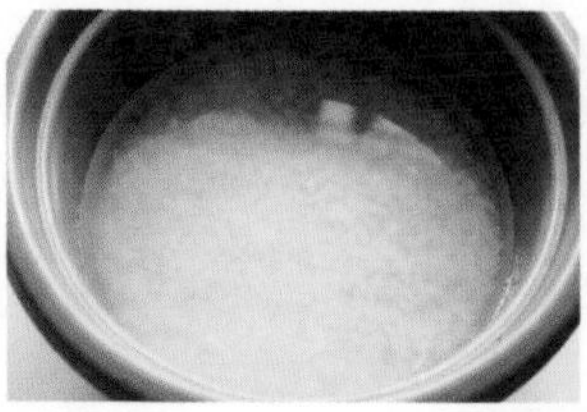

NOTES

- Use good quality rice for this dish to avoid the rice clumping up while cooking.
- Waste not, want not. My grandma adds the mushroom soaking liquid to the rice for an extra boost of flavour.
- Use yams that are light for their weight and which have a powdery texture. If in doubt, ask the vegetable seller at the market to help.

Fried Rice Vermicelli

Char Bee Hoon

Serves 2

This is the quintessential home-cooked dish in Singapore, a humble plate of rice vermicelli or *bee hoon*, stir-fried with strips of cabbage and carrot. A quick, one-wok wonder that has fed many a hungry tummy. This is my take on the dish, with the addition of dried mushrooms for texture and bulk, and fish sauce for that extra umami boost. You can also whisk up a couple of eggs, fry them into an omelette and cut it into strips to garnish the dish, like golden confetti, as Auntie Alicia used to do. This dish is also perfect to serve up when any vegetarians are in attendance — simply replace the fish sauce with more light soy sauce.

- 4–5 dried Chinese mushrooms
- 140 g dried rice vermicelli
- 180 g napa cabbage
- 2 Tbsp neutral-tasting oil such as canola or sunflower oil
- 3 garlic cloves, peeled and minced
- 1 carrot, peeled and cut into matchsticks
- ½ tsp sugar
- ½ tsp salt
- 1 Tbsp light soy sauce
- 1 Tbsp fish sauce
- 2 tsp dark soy sauce
- 1 tsp sesame oil
- A dash of ground white pepper

1. Soak the dried Chinese mushrooms in warm water for about 30 minutes or until softened. Squeeze excess water from the soaked mushrooms and measure the soaking liquid. Top it up with more water to make 200 ml. Set this water aside for use when stir-frying. Trim and discard the stems of the mushrooms, then slice the caps into strips. Set aside.
2. Soak the dried vermicelli in room temperature water for 10 minutes. Drain and set aside.
3. Cut the cabbage in half from top to bottom, then place it flat-side down and cut each half into chunks.
4. Heat the oil in a wok over high heat. When the oil is heated through, reduce the heat to low and add the garlic. Stir-fry until fragrant and lightly coloured. Add the mushrooms and stir-fry for about 1 minute.
5. Add the carrot and stir-fry for about 1 minute, before adding the cabbage. Crank the heat up to high and stir-fry the veggies until aromatic. Season with sugar and salt.
6. Add the rice vermicelli, mushroom soaking liquid, light soy sauce, fish sauce and dark soy sauce. Mix well, then cover the wok with a lid and let it cook for about a minute or so.
7. Remove the lid and give the vermicelli a stir. Check that the vermicelli is cooked. It should be soft but not mushy. If it is too dry, add a little more water to the wok and mix to allow the vermicelli to absorb the water.
8. Taste and adjust the seasoning with more light soy sauce and fish sauce if necessary. Turn off the heat.
9. Drizzle with sesame oil and finish with a dash of pepper before serving.

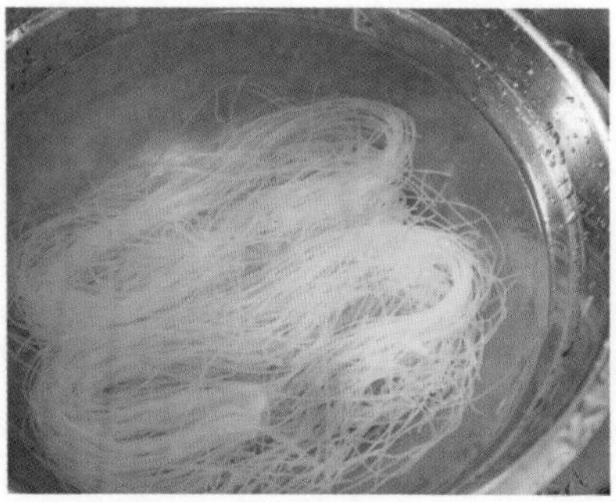

NOTES

- Soak the rice vermicelli in room temperature water for about 10 minutes to soften before cooking. Do not use hot water or soak for too long, or the rice vermicelli will become soft and mushy when cooked.
- I reserve the liquid from soaking the mushrooms and use it in place of plain water to add instant flavour to the dish.
- When stir-frying, take care not to be too aggressive or you may end up with short, broken strands of vermicelli. It happens to the best of us and the dish will still taste good, but it won't look as pretty.

Hokkien Prawn Mee Soup

Hae Mee Tng

Serves 4

Preparing this dish is truly a labour of love as it requires the prawn heads and shells to be carefully caramelised, patiently, then simmered slowly until the stock takes on an intense, rusty hue. All that work for just a few precious bowlfuls... for whoever you like best.

This is the sort of dish where you can tell the quality with just one look. A good prawn mee stock will be full-bodied with a reddish tint to it. Life is simply too short to settle for lacklustre, pallid-looking prawn mee soup. Make this.

600 g yellow mee, or a mixture of yellow mee and rice vermicelli
A handful of water spinach (*kangkong*)
2 fishcakes, sliced
A handful of bean sprouts
10–12 big prawns
Fried shallots (page 16) and/or lard croutons (page 16)

Stock
Canola or sunflower oil, as needed
400 g pork ribs
1 pig's tail
4 garlic cloves, peeled
1 onion, peeled and cut in half
40 g dried shrimps
300 g prawn heads and shells
2.5 litres water
1 star anise
1 cinnamon stick
3 dried red chillies
1 tsp white peppercorns
30 g rock sugar
¾ tsp salt, or to taste
2 Tbsp light soy sauce, or to taste

1. Prepare the stock. Heat 3 Tbsp oil in a wok over medium heat. Add the pork ribs and pig's tail and sear until lightly browned on all sides. This is to seal the ribs and tail to trap the impurities and add the first layer of flavour. Transfer to a big stockpot.
2. Reheat the wok. Add some oil if the wok looks dry. Add the garlic and onion and brown lightly. Transfer to the stockpot.
3. Soak the dried shrimps in water for about 15 minutes until softened. Drain, then stir-fry until golden brown. Transfer to the stockpot.
4. Add more oil to the wok if it looks dry. Add the prawn heads and shells and cook until they turn a deep reddish hue and are almost crisp. They should smell and look toasty. Transfer to the stockpot.
5. Fill the stockpot with the water. Add the star anise, cinnamon, dried red chillies, peppercorns and rock sugar. Bring to a boil, then reduce the heat and let it simmer over low heat for 2–3 hours, occasionally using the back of a wooden spoon to press down on the prawn heads and shells for them to release even more flavour into the stock.
6. Season with salt and light soy sauce, adjusting the flavour to your liking. Taste is subjective, and the flavour will also depend on how much water has evaporated and the amount of time spent boiling the stock. So feel free to add more salt, light soy sauce or sugar, until it is to your liking.
7. To serve, prepare a separate pot of boiling water. Add 150 g yellow mee and/or vermicelli and some water spinach to the boiling water. Turn off the heat and drain the entire mass. Arrange in a bowl. Top with some fishcake and bean sprouts. Repeat for each serving.
8. Return the stock to the boil. Add the prawns into the stock to cook through. This should take less than a minute. Drain the prawns and arrange on the noodles/water spinach. Ladle some stock through a strainer into each bowl. Garnish with fried shallots and/or lard croutons and serve!

NOTES

- When browning the ingredients for the stock, I typically use a neutral-tasting oil, but you can also use liquid lard (page 16) which is what the hawkers typically use.
- Whenever you cook prawns don't discard the precious heads and shells. Bag and stash them in the freezer for times like these. When you procure enough, you'll be able to make prawn mee for the gods.
- Caramelise, caramelise, caramelise. The key to this dish is to make sure your precious stash of prawn heads and shells gets justice by eliciting as much flavour from them as possible. Caramelise them till they are brown and toasty, and there is a rusty hued residue all over your cooking utensils. When you think it's ready, let it go on a bit further. You want a robust colour which can only be achieved by — you guessed it — caramelising the prawn shells well.
- The pig's tail and pork ribs lend body to the stock, giving it that rich mouthfeel.
- You can also pulverise the prawn heads and shells with the ready stock in a blender, then pass it through a strainer to extract maximum flavour from every inch of the prawns.

Fish Ball Noodle Soup

Kway Teow Tng

Serves 4

This is as easy to put together as it gets. You boil up some pork stock, season it, throw in some noodles of choice, some meat, maybe an egg, and you have yourself a meal. This is the quintessential Asian noodle soup with a mound of slippery noodles, bouncy fish balls and slices of fishcake. All over Asia, there's a version of this dish although it may not have been as widely exported as other noodle dishes. I top mine with tons of fried garlic to make it even more aromatic, and you could add fried shallots as well, or both. The key is to make sure you start off with a high quality, home-brewed pork stock. Store-bought stock would yield a completely different dish.

I use pork neck bones for the stock. If you're unsure what this is, go to your friendly neighbourhood butcher and tell him what you're making and what you're looking for. He'll take care of the rest. At the same time, pick up some freshly-made fish balls and flat rice noodles from the stall selling *yong tau foo* items and noodles, respectively.

250 ml pork stock
Cabbage leaves or any green leaves of choice
4–5 fish balls
A few slices of fishcake
150 g thin flat rice noodles (*kway teow*)
¼ tsp salt or to taste
1 tsp fried garlic and garlic oil (page 16)
A handful of coriander leaves

Pork Stock
(Makes about 1.5 litres)
500 g pork neck bones
1 big onion, peeled and cut in half
1.5 litres water

1. The pork stock can be prepared in advance and stored in the freezer. It will keep nicely in the freezer for a month or two days in the fridge.
2. Bring a pot of water to the boil and blanch the pork bones for 3–4 minutes to rid them of any scum and impurities. Rinse and drain. Discard the water.
3. Place the pork bones in a clean large stockpot. Add the onion and 1.5 litres water. Bring to the boil, then reduce to low heat and let it simmer for 1½–2 hours.
4. In a saucepan, bring 250 ml pork stock to the boil. Add the cabbage or green leaves, fish balls and slices of fishcake and let boil until the stock is heated through and the vegetables are soft.
5. Add the noodles and salt. Taste and adjust with more salt if necessary.
6. Transfer to a bowl and drizzle with fried garlic and garlic oil. Garnish with coriander leaves.

NOTES

- Using pork neck bones will ensure a less cloudy stock, which is what you're looking for in this style of soup.
- When boiling the stock, maintain a gentle simmer. Do not let it come to a vigorous boil. A harsh boil will only serve to make the soup murky, not what you want in this case.
- Pork neck bones contain a lot of collagen and when boiled over time, this breaks down into gelatine, which gives the stock depth of flavour and a rich mouthfeel, a certain viscosity, as compared to say, the plainness of water.
- Blanching the bones helps to remove any impurities and coagulate the surface proteins on the bones so they won't end up making the stock cloudy.
- This recipe is a good place to start if you are just starting to learn to cook. There's not much to do (save for the prep work and blanching the noodles) as the stock simmers and you're rewarded with a lovely, home-cooked meal thereafter.
- My favourite way to serve this is to top the dish with some fried garlic and its oil along with a sprinkling of coriander leaves and/or spring onions.

Handmade Noodles

Mee Hoon Kueh

Serves 4

These chewy, starchy noodles can be found in many food courts these days, their noodles perfectly regular. The ones here are perfectly imperfect — irregular and rough around the edges, a sign of being handmade and not processed by a piece of machinery, utterly devoid of character. Try making this at home at least once to understand that the commercial ones simply can't hold a candle to this version from Auntie Alicia. I have fond memories of returning home from school in the afternoons and being so excited whenever I spied the mound of dough sitting inside a bowl, covered with cling wrap to be pinched and added to the pot to cook a la minute.

A standard bowl of these noodles would feature flavourful, home-made stock, prawns, meatballs, fish balls and a generous lashing of freshly-fried anchovies. You take a piece of the wheat dough "noodle" and dip it in the ridiculously addictive concoction of minced garlic, sesame oil and light soy sauce. The bland noodle is the perfect foil to carry both the savoury stock and aromatic sauce. These do take a little bit of elbow grease if pulling the noodles for a large group, but once in a while, it makes for a great rainy day project and is well worth the effort.

8–12 small prawns
8–12 fish balls
Leafy greens such as bak choy or choy sum
3–4 Tbsp deep-fried anchovies
1 Tbsp fried shallots (page 16)
4 eggs

Anchovy Stock
100 g dried anchovies (*ikan bilis*)
2 litres water
1 big onion, peeled and cut in half
1 tsp salt, to taste

Dough
180 ml hot water
350 g plain flour

1. To prepare the stock, place all the ingredients in a saucepan and boil for 15–20 minutes. Strain and set aside.
2. To prepare the dough, stir the hot water into the flour in a bowl. Leave to sit until the dough is cool to the touch. Knead the dough until it comes together in a smooth ball, adjusting with more water or flour as needed. What you're looking for is a smooth dough that's ever so slightly tacky, but not sticky. Leave the dough aside to rest for an hour to relax the gluten. This will give the noodles a better texture.
3. Return the stock to the boil and add the prawns, fish balls and vegetables to cook.
4. Pinch rounds of the dough and flatten them, then toss them into the stock. Don't worry if the dough is a little rough around the edges — they're handmade and are meant to be like this. The noodles are cooked when they float to the top.
5. Crack an egg into each serving bowl and ladle the hot stock and ingredients over. Top with deep-fried anchovies and fried shallots.
6. Serve with a dipping sauce made from minced garlic, finely sliced bird's eye chillies, light soy sauce and sesame oil.

NOTES

- Using hot water gives the dough a springier texture, so don't substitute it in favour of room temperature water. Factor in some time to allow the hot mass of dough to cool before proceeding to knead it.
- When kneading, if the dough feels a little too stubborn to continue, let it sit to allow the gluten to relax. Go busy yourself with something else or take a tea break, then return to the kneading.
- You can make the stock and the fried anchovies a day ahead, leaving only the grease work of kneading, pinching and cooking the noodles on the day itself.
- The anchovy stock can be substituted with a vegetable stock made up of plenty of sweet root vegetables or a clear meat stock of your preference.

Pantry Noodles

Serves 1

These noodles are alarmingly easy to slurp up, each strand coated luxuriantly with the umami-rich sauce concoction given below. It is meant to be a quick-fix, when one needs a bowlful of carbs out pronto for emergency suppers. This is more of a guideline than a recipe, and most of the ingredients can be found in your typical pantry. Anything else that you can rummage for in your fridge can be an add-on, like frozen meatballs, eggs or just a sprinkling of spring onions stirred through the noodles. Speaking of, use just about any type of noodles you have on hand — thin or thick egg noodles, dried Japanese noodles, anything that strikes your fancy, really. My cousin's favourite version of this dish is made with the handmade noodles (page 32) that Auntie Alicia very expertly pulls into stretchy curtains. When you make those noodles, do save some of the dough to try this out.

What makes this taste so ridiculously addictive is the use of the home-made dried shrimp sambal (page 17) which lends an incredibly rich, spicy and sweet flavour to the noodles. When the hot noodles hit the sauce, the heat enlivens its flavours, releasing all the aromas from within.

140 g dried noodles or for freshly-made noodles, use about 200 g
Any add-ons
Spring onions or fried shallots (page 16)

Sauce
1½ Tbsp dried shrimp sambal (page 17) or substitute with any store-bought sauce with tons of chilli and dried seafood
1½ tsp light soy sauce
1 tsp dark soy sauce
1 Tbsp sesame oil, shallot oil or garlic oil (page 16)

1. Cook the instant noodles in boiling water according to the instructions on the pack. If you want any add-ons, drop them into the boiling water at this point to cook alongside the noodles.
2. While the noodles are cooking, mix the ingredients for the sauce up in the serving bowl.
3. When the noodles are done to your liking, use a strainer to remove them from the cooking liquid and drop them into the serving bowl. Mix it up.
4. Top with spring onions or fried shallots and slurp up!

NOTES

- If you don't want to go through the trouble of frying dried shrimp sambal from ground zero, you could just as easily use a good quality jar of crispy prawn chilli or XO sauce from the store. Read the ingredient list and test if you like the flavour of it. The punchy ones would have some dried seafood in their making.

“One cannot think well, love well
sleep well, if one has not dined well.”

~ Virginia Woolf

Around the Dining Table

Freshly steamed whole fish topped with shards of ginger, just out the wok that doubles as a steamer; a colourful medley of vegetables given a quick blast in the wok; steamed eggs so custardy, their pillowy softness the perfect foil for steamed white rice, a bowl of soup, brewed for hours with pork bones and brimming with goodies like Chinese wolfberries, red dates, lotus root and dried scallops, promising to nourish the body after a long day's toil.

When the Chinese talk about having a meal, they use the phrase "*chi fan*", which literally means "eat rice." To greet others, one may also ask "*ni chi fan le ma?*" which translates to "have you eaten rice?" highlighting the importance of the grain to the Chinese.

Besides being a symbol of eating well, rice also symbolises the coming together of every member of the household, supping around the dining table at the end of their day. A bowl of steamed rice for every person, with several dishes laid out on the dining table, bringing us back to the concept of "three dishes one soup" (*san cai yi tang*). It's amazing how quickly Chinese home cooks are able to dole out multiple dishes of family favourites, then leave the kitchen spick and span by the time we get home, leaving no trace of the frenzy that must have ensued during cooking. A home-cooked meal like this is a luxury.

Even though the term is "three dishes one soup", you can very well use any variation or number of dishes you fancy in this section to make up your nourishing meal. If you're short on time, just two dishes would happily suffice. If you want to go the full blowout, you could choose one dish of every variety along with a soup. Mix and match. Vary it up. Do what suits your schedule or mood best. Life has enough constraining elements, cooking should not be one of them...

Steamed Minced Pork with Salted Egg

Serves 4–6 as part of a meal

A slab of steamed, grey meat isn't going to win any beauty contests, but as the aphorism goes, let's not go judging a book by its cover. There are many ways to go about this giant patty of steamed meat, which is usually paired with condiments that provide a punch, such as salted fish, salted radish, fermented black beans or salted egg, all with the potential to make steamed meat exciting.

You can choose to use ready minced pork or hand chop your own, in any case, just make sure you've got a good amount of fat in your pork mince. The water chestnuts add sweetness and crunch to the patty, which is perfumed with ginger and spring onion, aromatics that help to cut through any strong meaty smells. After steaming, the fragrant pork will release some of its flavourful juices, making it perfect to drizzle atop steamed white rice.

- 2 dried Chinese mushrooms or a few pieces of dried black fungus
- 3 water chestnuts
- 200 g minced pork
- 4 spring onions, finely sliced
- ½ tsp grated or finely chopped ginger
- A good dash of ground white pepper
- 1 tsp sesame oil
- 1 tsp light soy sauce
- ½ tsp sugar
- ½ tsp Shaoxing rice wine
- 1 salted egg, yolk and white separated
- 2 Tbsp water

1. Soak the dried Chinese mushrooms or dried black fungus in warm water for about 30 minutes or until softened. If using mushrooms, squeeze the excess water from the mushrooms, then trim and discard their tough, woody stems. Cut the caps into small cubes. If using black fungus, drain and cut into small cubes. Discard any hard bits.
2. Wash the water chestnuts, then peel and cut them into small cubes.

3. In a bowl, mix the minced pork together with the spring onions, ginger, pepper, sesame oil, light soy sauce, sugar, rice wine, salted egg white and water chestnuts. Using a pair of chopsticks, stir in one direction to combine the ingredients into a homogeneous mass, allowing the meat to be infused with the aromatics. Continue stirring vigorously until the mixture lightens in colour and feels tender, or less of a stodgy mass than when it started out. This is a result of the egg white working to bind everything together. Slowly incorporate about 2 Tbsp water into the meat mixture, stirring continuously.
4. Transfer the mixture to a shallow heatproof plate and spread it out evenly so it covers the base of the plate. Make a shallow indentation in the middle of the patty and place the salted egg yolk on top, either whole or chopped into pieces.
5. If there is time, allow the pork to sit in the marinade for a few minutes before steaming. Otherwise, proceed to steam over medium-high heat for 5–8 minutes, or until the pork is completely cooked through.
6. Remove the plate from the steamer and adorn the meat patty with more spring onions, chopped chillies or ginger. Serve with rice or porridge (page 15).

NOTES

- Salted eggs are duck eggs that have been preserved in brine, resulting in a golden yolk with a powdery texture and a pristine white that's almost like a salty agar. Some come ready cooked, but in this recipe, make sure to use the uncooked ones.
- Use pork shoulder or pork belly for this, or a mixture of lean meat and fat. Basically, you can use any permutation you desire as long as there's some fat and it's not all lean meat. The fat will help make for a more tender patty.
- The water chestnuts and aromatics are not only to flavour the pork mince. They aid in the tenderising process of the meat patty as well.
- If mincing your own meat, freeze it for 10 minutes or so before starting the chopping process. To mince, cut the meat into thin slices, then into tiny little cubes. Once the tiny cubes are formed, roughly chop and mash the entire mass together so they form a slightly sticky paste.
- Honestly, I get cranky if hand mincing a large quantity of meat. My solution is then to hand-mince a portion of the meat and mix it with ready minced meat.

Ginger Pork

Serves 4–6 as part of a meal

This is a perennial crowd-pleaser that is incredibly easy and quick to put together. It features thin slices of tender pork, coated with a sweet and salty sauce, mixed with strips of ginger, its glowing warmth permeating every bite. A final flourish of sesame oil and Shaoxing rice wine towards the end of cooking helps bring out the flavours.

200 g pork tenderloin or shoulder
1 Tbsp light soy sauce
1½ Tbsp dark soy sauce
Sesame oil, as needed
1 tsp cornstarch
10 g ginger, peeled and cut into matchsticks
1 Tbsp Shaoxing rice wine (optional)
1 spring onion, finely sliced

1. Cut the meat into thin slices across the grain. Place in a bowl and season with the soy sauces, 1 tsp sesame oil and cornstarch. Set aside for about 10 minutes.
2. Place a wok over medium-high heat. Add 1½ Tbsp sesame oil and give it a swirl to coat the surface of the wok.
3. Add the ginger and stir-fry until it is fragrant and lightly browned. This may take 1–2 minutes depending on the heat of the wok.
4. Add the meat and stir-fry for about a minute until almost cooked through. Add the rice wine, if using, drizzling it in from the side of the wok and allowing it to evaporate as it heats up. Turn off the heat and add the spring onion.
5. Dish out and serve.

NOTES

- You can use young or mature ginger in this dish. Young ginger has thinner, lighter skin compared to mature ginger. It is less fibrous and can be consumed as part of the dish. Mature ginger is more pungent and is typically added for its flavour.
- You can use pork tenderloin (*you bak*) to prepare this dish. It is a pricier cut, but it is incredibly tender and will work well in this stir-fry.
- The cornstarch is used to form a protective layer around the meat, sealing in its juices and flavour as it cooks, giving the meat a tender, silky feel.

Sesame Chicken

Serves 4–6 as part of a meal

Thin matchsticks of ginger sizzling in nutty, amber-hued sesame oil in a clay pot on the stove, slowly darkening around the edges as they cook. A splash of Shaoxing rice wine, imbuing the dish with a ghost of its flavour. All the classic ingredients in this dish — ginger, sesame oil and rice wine — are energy-giving components, making it the perfect antidote for balmy evenings or when one has a cold. This is also great for mothers in confinement, helping to restore their energy spent during childbirth. The sesame oil really enhances the sweetness of the chicken and the resulting sauce can be drizzled over steamed white rice, or be used as a base for soup. The addition of Chinese wolfberries is optional, but a great way to amp up the nutrition content. It also adds a trickle of sweetness to the dish.

1 kampong/free range chicken, about 1 kg, cleaned
1 Tbsp grated young ginger
2 Tbsp oyster sauce
2 tsp cornstarch
8 dried Chinese mushrooms
40 g mature ginger
4 Tbsp sesame oil
2 Tbsp Shaoxing rice wine
3 Tbsp light soy sauce
1½ Tbsp Chinese wolfberries
½ tsp salt or to taste

1. Cut off the head and neck of the chicken and trim the tips of the claws from the feet. Chop the chicken into 8–10 pieces. Alternatively, get the butcher to do this for you.
2. Rinse the chicken and place in a big bowl. Add the grated young ginger, oyster sauce and cornstarch. Mix well and set aside.
3. Soak the dried Chinese mushrooms in warm water for about 30 minutes or until softened. Squeeze excess water from the soaked mushrooms and measure the soaking liquid. Top it up with more water to make 400 ml. Set this water aside for adding to the stew. Trim and discard the stems of the mushrooms, then cut the caps into large chunks.
4. Peel the mature ginger, then cut it into thin slices before cutting again into matchsticks.
5. Place a clay pot or stewing pot over low heat. Add the sesame oil and let it heat up for a few seconds.
6. Add the mature ginger and allow the flavours to infuse. When fragrant and the edges of the ginger start to colour and curl, add the mushrooms. Stir-fry lightly, then add the chicken.
7. Let the chicken sear lightly, then crank the heat up to high and add the rice wine and light soy sauce. Stir-fry to mix and allow the wine to evaporate. This should take about a minute or so.
8. Add the mushroom soaking liquid, Chinese wolfberries and salt. Cover the pot with a lid and let it simmer over low heat for 15–20 minutes, or until the chicken is cooked through and tender.
9. At this point, you can remove the lid and reduce the liquid further to your desired consistency. Taste and adjust the seasoning as necessary.

NOTES

- Young ginger has thin, delicate skin and is less fibrous than mature ginger. Its flavour is also not as harsh as mature ginger. The mature ginger gives this dish its requisite kick. A variety known as *wen dong* ginger is typically used for its stronger flavour.
- Kampong or free range chicken has less fat, being allowed to roam free instead of being cooped up and fed with antibiotics. For cooking soups and stews, my parents have a preference for the healthier kampong or free range chicken.
- I usually get the butcher to chop the chicken up into stewing pieces. You can do this yourself if you have the dexterity to hack through bones.
- Use bone-in chicken as it is the bones that will help flavour the stew. You can also use chicken thigh meat. Note that breast meat will inevitably turn out more stringy.
- Adjust the liquid content of the dish to your preference. If you want it more soupy, add more water. If you want it slightly thicker, let the liquid boil down towards the end of cooking, with the pot uncovered. Just be sure to taste and adjust the seasoning accordingly.

Grandpa Zhang's Fried Chicken Wings

Serves 4–6 as part of a meal

This is a last minute addition to the book, a tribute to my paternal grandpa who just has a natural flair in the kitchen. I wanted to document this somewhere, so that this small part of his legacy lives on. His memory has been failing him lately due to illness, and along with it, many more recipes, ideas and the people he holds dear. This is my way of getting to know him, through the stories my dad tells me and through tasting this — his famous fried chicken wings. Back in the day, he ran a stall in a coffee shop selling these crunchy, double-coated wings. He had his fair share of fans, one of them being a tubby young boy who would demand that his mother buy him two wings daily, else he would kick up a tantrum ending in waterworks. My grandpa would muse cheekily that he could fry up wings better than a certain white-haired colonel could. I've tasted the wings and verified that statement to be true. That breading of flaky biscuit crumbs is really key to this.

10 whole chicken wings
4 garlic cloves, peeled and minced
6 shallots, peeled and minced
1 Tbsp light soy sauce
1½ tsp salt
Ground white pepper, to taste
1 Tbsp sesame oil
About 150 g plain flour
About 15 cream crackers, finely crushed
2 eggs

1. Place the chicken with the garlic, shallots, light soy sauce, salt, a dash of pepper and sesame oil in a big bowl. Mix well, cover and set aside. Let the chicken marinate for at least a couple of hours to let the seasoning soak in.
2. Set up your breading station. Tip the plain flour onto a plate. On another plate, place the crushed cream crackers. Beat the eggs in a bowl.
3. The process goes like this: Take a chicken wing, dip it in the egg mixture, then coat it with the biscuit crumbs followed by the flour. Set aside. Repeat with the remaining chicken wings.
4. Heat sufficient oil for deep-frying over medium heat or use an air-fryer/deep-fryer if you have one. Fry the chicken in batches to avoid over-crowding, until the skin is crisp and golden brown. Drain well and enjoy! This is best eaten with fingers. I should warn you though, these don't stay crisp the entire day, so they are best eaten straight out of the fryer, but that shouldn't be a problem!

NOTES

- When using this recipe, my dad uses the entire wing which includes the drumette attached to the wingette and tip, so the measurements provided here are for that. If you prefer a particular cut, adjust the recipe accordingly. Either getting double the amount of that particular cut, say drumettes only, or reducing the amount of seasoning.
- When deep-frying, make sure you use sufficient oil to submerge the chicken pieces. The oil should also be hot enough such that when you drop the chicken in, it sizzles and bubbles. If it is a calm ripple, the oil isn't hot enough.
- Use those old-school cream crackers for these, not fancy digestives or butter biscuits. There is just something about those flaky, salty, crunchy biscuits that makes them so good!

Steamed Fish with Fermented Soy Beans

Serves 4–6 as part of a meal

This is one of the best ways to have fish, steamed with fermented soy bean paste (*tau cheo*) that packs a huge flavour punch. I was one of those kids extremely averse to steamed fish. Their slimy, silvery skin was enough to send chills down my spine. I had to be cajoled and coerced into getting my dose of omega-3 and protein during dinners. But this was the only form of steamed fish I gladly consumed. The fermented soy bean paste infused with the trinity of Chinese aromatics — garlic, ginger and chilli — sautéed until golden and fragrant. The resulting paste is spread on the fish and steamed briefly over high heat, resulting in perfectly perfumed and tender white flesh, encased by a pool of this amazingly pungent (I mean that in a good way) sauce. Even after all these years, I still get blown away by the flavours of this simple steamed fish whenever my grandma makes it for us.

1 small grouper, about 350 g
1 Tbsp sesame oil
10 g mature ginger, peeled and finely minced
1 garlic clove, peeled and finely minced
1 red bird's eye chilli, finely minced
45 g fermented soy bean paste (*tau cheo*)

1. Start by preparing the fish. Ensure that the fish is cleaned, scaled and thoroughly washed. Make 2 slits on each side of the fish for more even heat distribution during cooking. Set aside while preparing the sauce.
2. Place a wok over low heat and add the sesame oil. Let it gradually heat up for about 1 minute. Add the minced ginger and fry until lightly golden brown, stirring occasionally to ensure even browning.
3. Add the minced garlic and bird's eye chilli, letting the aromatics flavour the oil. Fry until golden brown and incredibly fragrant.
4. Add the fermented soy bean paste and let the entire mass cook, allowing the flavours to be released and to mingle with one another. Cook for 2–3 minutes and turn off the heat.
5. Prepare the steaming vessel. I usually use a large stainless steel wok with a lid and place a steaming rack in the centre. Fill with water. The water level should not be higher than the rack. Turn on high heat.
6. Prepare a heatproof plate that will fit into the steaming vessel. A plate with slightly rounded sides will work best to house all the resulting juices.
7. Smear the fermented soy bean paste mixture evenly on both sides of the fish. Place the fish on the prepared plate and on the rack. Cover the wok and steam over medium-high heat for 7–8 minutes, or until the prongs of a fork or chopstick goes through the flesh without any resistance. By this time, a pool of fragrant sauce from both the aromatic paste and steaming juices will have formed around the fish. Perfect with rice.

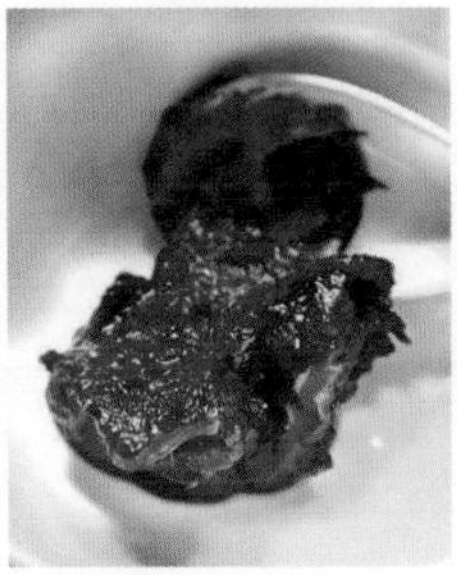

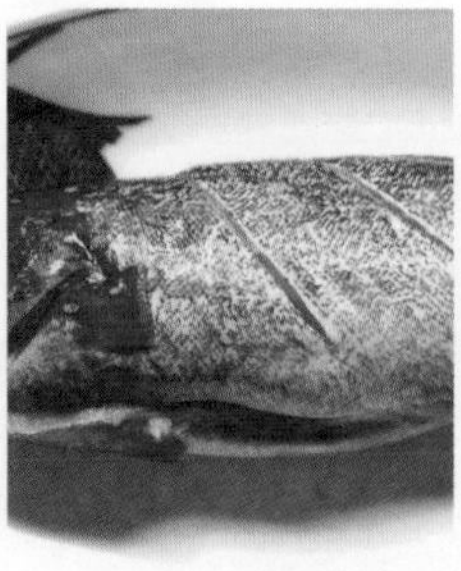

NOTES

- This fermented soy bean paste has a strong, salty, pungent and almost yeasty aroma. A little goes a long way with this intense condiment, so use sparingly. It adds another dimension of savouriness that's more than just salty, which is what makes this dish taste so good.
- There are many types of fermented soy bean paste, ranging from light brown to a dark shade teetering on black. There are also smooth purées or those with the beans left almost intact. Experiment and see which ones you prefer. The darker pastes can be found in wet markets. These usually come with some chilli and garlic already added and they tend to be a little less salty.
- I usually go to a trusted stall at the wet market, select my fish and get the fish monger to scale and gut the fish for me. This leaves me to just trim the tail and any sharp fins and give the fish a good rinse.
- If you want the final dish to have more sauce, splash some water over the fish before steaming.
- You know the fish is done when its eyes become opaque and pop out, and a fork pierced into the fish meets with no resistance.

Teochew-style Steamed Pomfret

Serves 4–6 as part of a meal

This traditional style of steamed fish relies on the use of numerous sour and salty elements, like pickled sour plums, preserved mustard greens and juicy wedges of tomato, ingredients that will help cut through any fishy aromas. Truth be told, I was never a fan of this dish growing up and I avoided eating it at all costs. I've since transitioned into adulthood with an ever-expanding appetite for all sorts of food. The appeal of this dish is now also clear — how the preserved ingredients perk up the sauce with their bracing bite, adding that tinge of sourness that partners pleasantly with the seafood.

1 silver pomfret, about 500 g
3 dried Chinese mushrooms
20 g mature ginger
1 tsp salt
1 tsp light soy sauce
1 tomato, cut into 8 wedges or 8–10 cherry tomatoes, halved
50 g salted mustard greens, cut into thin strips
1 red bird's eye chilli, thinly sliced
2 pickled sour plums
A dash of Shaoxing rice wine

1. Prepare the fish. Wash and clean the fish inside out. Trim the tail and the fins. Ensure that the fish can fit snugly onto your steaming plate. After the fish has been thoroughly cleaned, make 2 slits on each side of the fish. This will allow the fish to be cooked through to the bone more easily.
2. Soak the dried Chinese mushrooms in warm water for about 30 minutes or until softened. Squeeze excess water from the soaked mushrooms and reserve the soaking liquid. Trim and discard the stems, then slice the caps into strips. Set aside.
3. Peel the ginger, then cut it into thin slices before cutting again into matchsticks. Set aside.
4. Rub the salt and light soy sauce evenly over the fish and place it on the steaming plate. Arrange the tomato wedges or cherry tomato halves, mushroom slices, salted mustard greens, bird's eye chilli and ginger on and around the fish. Using your hands, tear up the sour plums and scatter the pieces over the fish.
5. Drizzle about 4 Tbsp mushroom soaking liquid and some Shaoxing rice wine over the fish. Let the fish sit in this marinade for about 10 minutes to allow some of the flavours to penetrate the flesh.
6. Prepare the steaming vessel. I usually use a large stainless steel wok with a lid and place a steaming rack in the centre. Fill with water. The water level should not be higher than the rack. Turn on high heat.
7. Prepare a heatproof plate that will fit into the steaming vessel. A plate with slightly rounded sides will work best to house all the resulting juices.
8. Place the fish on the prepared plate and on the rack. Cover the wok and steam over high heat for 6–8 minutes, then turn off the heat. Let the fish rest inside the steaming vessel for about 2 minutes.
9. Serve with rice.

NOTES

- When buying pomfret, note that silver pomfret is ideal for steaming while black pomfret is more suitable for frying.
- If you like your steamed fish on the saucy side, add a touch more of the mushroom-soaking liquid prior to steaming.
- Soak the salted mustard greens for about 10 minutes before using to rid them of any excess saltiness.

Sweet and Sour Prawns

Serves 4–6 as part of a meal

There are many fancy versions of sweet sour anything. Growing up, Auntie Alicia always made sweet and sour fish, prawns and pork, the protein deep-fried until golden before being cloaked in the sauce. The key to this is to properly deep-fry the protein, in this case, the prawns, allowing for an intensification of their natural flavours. Have you smelled your kitchen when shell-on prawns are being fried? I am honestly not a huge fan of deep-frying, but it makes all the difference here. The sweet and sour component couldn't be simpler and it comes straight out of the bottle in the form of tomato ketchup. Anything tastes better to a child when spiked with that sweet red goo. I make no apologies for the simplicity of the sauce for it is the stuff I grew up eating, and it tastes pretty damn good which is all that matters when you're feeding loved ones. This is just what it is. A simple, incredibly tasty home-cooked dish.

- 500 g medium prawns, shells on
- 125 g tomato ketchup
- ¼ tsp sugar
- ¼ tsp salt
- Cooking oil for deep-frying
- ½ yellow onion, peeled and cut into large chunks
- 1 green capsicum, cored and cut into chunks

1. Start by preparing the prawns. Trim the long feelers and the sharp pointy bit above their eyes. Then, using scissors, make a cut down the back of each prawn through the shell and remove the greenish intestinal tract. Give the prawns a good rinse and pat dry.
2. Mix the ketchup with the sugar and salt. Set aside.
3. Place a wok/pan over medium heat and add sufficient oil for deep-frying. How much oil to use would depend on the height and width of your vessel — you're looking for the prawns to be just about submerged under the oil.
4. When the oil is heated through, add the prawns. You just want to cook them lightly — the prawns should curl up slightly and have a good colour around the edges of their shells.
5. When done, remove the prawns and place them on a plate lined with kitchen paper to soak up any excess oil. (The oil that you just fried the prawns in will take on a copper hue, forming a prawn-infused oil. Save this precious oil for future use, say as the base for making a simple noodle stir-fry or for a seafood stew.)
6. Heat about 2 Tbsp of the oil used for deep-frying the prawns in a wok over medium heat. Add the onion and green capsicum. Stir-fry for about 20 seconds, then add the ketchup mixture to warm it up.
7. Add the deep-fried prawns and quickly toss to coat them with the sauce. Turn off the heat, taste and adjust the seasoning as necessary.
8. Dish out and serve.

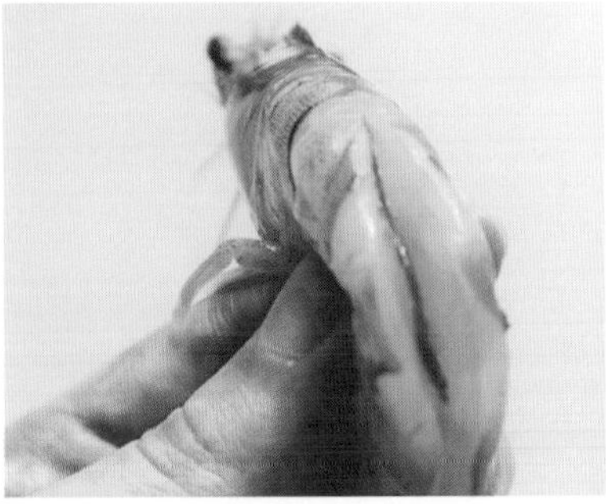

NOTES

- The initial step of deep-frying the prawns is what intensifies their flavour. Through frying, the prawn shells are burnished and lend another layer of flavour to the final dish versus merely pan-frying. It is much more work though, with the possibility of the oil splattering from any hint of moisture from the ingredients. I'm thankful for the air-fryer which makes life significantly easier, but if you don't have one, a splatter guard or a makeshift cardboard shield would be your best friend in this situation!
- Use whatever capsicums you prefer — red, green or yellow. I specify green only because that's what Auntie Alicia usually uses.

Cereal Prawns

Mai Pian Xia

Serves 4–6 as part of a meal

Sizzling butter (a good quality one, of course, not butter-flavoured anything or margarine), infused with the aromatic warmth of tiny, green curry leaves and sliced bird's eye chilli. A cereal mix that soaks up all the butter like a sponge, taking on a bronzed golden crunch and coating the prawns. All salty, slightly sweet and with a kick of heat, the familiar fragrance we now know too well thanks to the craze of salted egg yolk snacks. My family used to enjoy these cereal prawns all the time at our favourite *tze char* (cooked food) stall, but they started to skimp on the butter, causing the dish to lose its fragrance over the years. Here, you can be as generous with the butter and cereal coating as your heart desires — cos let's be frank, the true star of this dish is the cereal, not the prawns...

300 g medium prawns
1 tsp salt
1½ Tbsp potato starch
Vegetable or canola oil for deep-frying

Cereal Coating
50 g cereal drink mix
1½ Tbsp milk powder
¾ tsp salt
3 tsp sugar
6 sprigs curry leaves
60 g unsalted butter
1 bird's eye chilli, thinly sliced

1. Start by preparing the prawns. Trim the long feelers and the sharp pointy bit above their eyes. Then, using scissors, make a cut down the back of each prawn through the shell and remove the green intestinal tract (see page 50). Give the prawns a good rinse and pat dry.
2. Sprinkle the salt and potato starch evenly over the cleaned prawns.
3. Place a wok/pan over medium heat and add sufficient oil for deep-frying. How much oil to use would depend on the height and width of your vessel — you're looking for the prawns to be just about submerged under the oil.
4. When the oil is heated through, add half the prawns. The prawns are done when they become golden with a slight crunch to their appearance. When done, remove the prawns and place them on a plate lined with kitchen paper to soak up any excess oil. Repeat to cook the remaining prawns.
5. In a bowl, combine the cereal drink mix, milk powder, salt and sugar.
6. Strip the curry leaves from the stalks. Set them aside.
7. Drain the oil from the wok/pan. Add the butter and let it melt over low heat. Add the curry leaves and chilli and fry for about 40 seconds, allowing their fragrance to be released.
8. Tip in the cereal drink mix, stirring continuously. The cereal will absorb the butter and start to toast. When the cereal is lightly golden, add the prawns and coat evenly. Turn off the heat and dish out to a serving plate, making sure to get every last bit of the cereal out!

NOTES

- The Chinese name of this dish, "*mai pian xia*", is literally "oatmeal prawns", but what is used to give the requisite crunch and texture iconic of this dish is actually a cereal drink mix. The addition of some milk powder provides a boost of flavour and adds a tinge of sweetness.
- Instead of plucking the curry leaves from the stalk one by one, hold the thicker end of the stalk with one hand and using your other hand, run your thumb and forefinger down the length of the stalk. The leaves should come off easily.
- Be careful not to burn the cereal when toasting it. It can go from golden and crunchy to black and acrid in mere moments. To avoid this, watch it like a hawk and stir continuously over low heat. When the desired colour is achieved, quickly toss in the prawns, coat and turn, then remove to a serving plate to prevent any overcooking or burning.

Steamed Garlic Prawns

Serves 4–6 as part of a meal

The recipe for this dish comes from my friend, Lennard, who happens to be a kitchen wizard, a finalist in MasterChef Asia and a talented home cook who churns out dishes that could put professional kitchens to shame. There is so much going on in this dish, in a simple and good way. It's the layering of flavours in each step, producing a final taste that creates a symphony in your mouth. The prawns are first marinated in Shaoxing rice wine and light soy sauce. The glass noodles are given a soak in prawn oil. The seasoning mixture is then cooked with an obscene amount of garlic. All these disparate elements are then united on a plate for their final steam-bath. This dish will make any diner happy, so thanks to Lennard for sharing this!

10 big prawns
2 Tbsp Shaoxing rice wine
Light soy sauce, as needed
40 g dried glass noodles
2 Tbsp sesame oil
10 garlic cloves, peeled and minced
A bunch of spring onions
+ more for garnishing

Prawn Oil
4 Tbsp canola oil
Prawn shells

1. Start by peeling the shell from the body of the prawns. Rinse and reserve the shells for making the prawn oil. Keep the tails and heads on. Make a slit down the back of the bodies and remove the greenish intestinal tract (see page 50). Give the prawns a good rinse and drain well.
2. Place the prawns in a deep dish and drizzle with the Shaoxing rice wine and 1 Tbsp light soy sauce. Set aside to marinate.
3. Soak the glass noodles in warm water for 5 minutes. Drain.
4. Prepare the prawn oil. Heat the canola oil in a saucepan over medium heat. Add the prawn shells and let cook until the oil is flavoured and takes on a reddish hue. It will take just a couple of minutes and you will smell it.
5. Drizzle 2 Tbsp of this prawn oil over the glass noodles, along with ½ Tbsp light soy sauce.
6. Prepare a garlic sauce. Remove and discard the prawn shells from the saucepan of oil. To the remaining prawn oil, add the sesame oil and minced garlic. Let it simmer over low heat for a couple of minutes. You just want to cook off the raw taste of the garlic without letting it brown. Turn off the heat and drizzle in 1 Tbsp light soy sauce. Add the bunch of spring onions.
7. Place the glass noodles in the centre of a steaming plate. Arrange the prawns around the glass noodles in a single layer. Drizzle the garlic sauce evenly over the prawns and glass noodles. Place in a steamer and steam over medium heat for 3–5 minutes, until the prawns are just cooked through. The timing will depend on the size of the prawns.
8. Garnish with a final flourish of chopped spring onions and serve!

Chilli Squid

Sambal Sotong

Serves 4–6 as part of a meal

Tender curls of squid with just the slightest bite, draped with a home-made chilli sauce, infused with whole lemongrass and kaffir lime leaves, imparting a touch of their sprightly, citrusy aromas, instead of a full-on immersion. A haunting note lingering in the background you can't quite place your finger on. It's there but not there, making it all the more intriguing. This is the way my dad, a naturally gifted cook (see page 83 on my dad's pineapple tarts), prepares his squid. As they cook in the hot wok, the pieces of squid will release their natural saline juices to emulsify with the chilli sauce, boosting its flavour. Imagine instant seafood stock added to the wok. It is thus essential to use extremely fresh squid. It would be a crime not to serve this with freshly steamed rice to soak up the sauce, as rice is the perfect vehicle that allows the flavourful sauce to shine even brighter.

800 g squid, about 2 big ones
4–5 kaffir lime leaves
2 stalks lemongrass
1 big onion, peeled and sliced
4 Tbsp chilli sauce (recipe follows), or to taste
2 Tbsp cooking oil

Chilli Sauce
150 g shallots, peeled
50 g garlic, peeled
11 big red chillies
4–5 bird's eye chillies
240 ml cooking oil
4 tsp sugar
1 tsp salt

1. Prepare the chilli sauce. Roughly chop the shallots and garlic. Make a slit down the middle of the big red chillies and remove the seeds. Use gloves to prevent your hands from burning. You can do the same with the bird's eye chillies. I usually leave the seeds in.
2. Using a small food processor (or blender or mortar and pestle), purée one-fifth of the aromatics together first. You want them to turn liquid before adding the rest of the ingredients. Blend until a smooth, red purée forms.
3. When ready, heat the oil in a wok over medium heat. Add the purée and stir constantly, making sure to scrape the bottom of the wok to prevent any scorching of the ingredients. The paste is ready when it is aromatic, has turned a darker shade and a layer of oil has risen to the top. This should take about 8 minutes. Add the sugar and salt. Taste and adjust the seasoning if necessary. This recipe makes enough for two portions (1.6 kg) of squid. Any excess can be stored in a clean, airtight container in the fridge.
4. To clean the squid, separate the tentacles from the body. Cut away and discard the portion with the eyes, beak and ink sac. Pull the quill (the part that looks like a piece of plastic) from inside the squid. Rinse the squid tube thoroughly. Peel away the purple skin to reveal the opaque white flesh.
5. Cut the squid tube open and lay it out flat on the cutting board. Score it gently with diagonal cuts. Be careful not to cut all the way through the flesh. Repeat to score it the other way to create a criss-cross pattern. This will allow the squid to curl and bloom beautifully when cooked.
6. Cut the squid tube into chunky pieces roughly 3–4-cm wide. Having them about the same size will ensure that they cook more evenly.
7. Using your hands, tear the kaffir lime leaves to release some of its flavour.
8. Peel and discard the tough outer layers of the lemongrass, then trim the top end. You only want the tender bulbous stem. Use the back of a knife or a rolling pin and smash the lemongrass stems to bruise them and release their flavour.
9. Heat the oil in a wok over medium heat. Add the kaffir lime leaves, lemongrass and onion. Allow the flavours to infuse the oil. When fragrant, toss in the squid. Give it a good stir to allow the squid to release its liquids. After 1–2 minutes, add 4 Tbsp chilli sauce. Stir to help everything emulsify. The dish is ready when the squid is opaque and the sauce has thickened and coats every piece of squid and onion.
10. Dish out and enjoy with rice.

NOTES

- Chop up the garlic, shallots and chilli into rough chunks to make for easier blending.
- If you want a spicier sauce, leave the seeds in or add more bird's eye chillies. My dad sometimes prepares this using only the tiny, feisty chillies, but it's reserved for chilli fiends. The fiery heat will not appeal to regular taste buds!
- To purée the ingredients, I find a tiny food processor does the job best. My dad and grandma use the blender, but that would require the addition of a little water to enable everything to come together smoothly, and I prefer not to have added water.
- When using a food processor, blend a small amount of the aromatics first, then allow the initial batch to liquidise before adding the rest of the ingredients. I find this helps make blending easier.
- If you do not want to go through the trouble of cooking your own chilli, you could use store-bought chilli sauce. Just make sure it is a trusted brand.
- This recipe for chilli sauce can be used for almost anything — spread over prawns or fish, then baked or steamed, or added to spice up a vegetable stir-fry.

Steamed Three-egg Custard

Serves 4–6 as part of a meal

Steamed eggs served with piping hot watery porridge — the grain still visible — crunchy pickles, steamed minced pork and perhaps canned fried dace fragrant with fermented black beans. I remember these dishes laid out on the dining table, protected by a large mesh screen food cover that kept the flies away in the afternoon heat. Coming home to a lovingly prepared meal, all the effort put forth beforehand, then laid out, awaiting your return. It is a sight to behold, to cherish.

These salty, flavourful dishes are the perfect accompaniments to the plainness of the rice porridge. All very comforting and easy to slurp down. When properly steamed, the egg custard is softly-set and smooth, with the little jewelled cuts of the gleaming black century eggs and pristine white salted eggs scattered throughout.

2 eggs
150 ml hot water or stock of your heart's desire
A dash of ground white pepper
1 tsp light soy sauce
1 tsp shallot oil (page 16)
1 century egg, peeled and cut into tiny cubes
½ cooked salted egg, peeled and cut into tiny cubes

1. Whisk the eggs with the hot water or stock, pepper, light soy sauce and shallot oil until just combined. Strain the mixture through a fine mesh sieve into a shallow heatproof bowl for steaming.
2. Scatter the century and salted eggs to spread them out in the egg mixture. Cover the bowl with aluminium foil and place in a steamer.
3. Steam using the lowest setting possible. It should take 10–12 minutes. When you remove the foil and jiggle the bowl, the steamed egg will wobble slightly and be barely set. You don't want overcooked, tough protein, so err on the side of caution!
4. Serve with rice porridge (page 15).

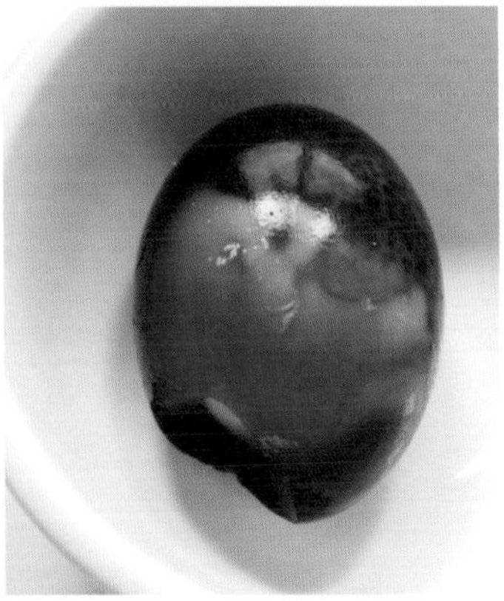

What are century eggs?

Contrary to what their name implies, century eggs have not been left sitting around for a thousand years. They are made by curing duck eggs in a thick alkali mixture until the whites turn translucent black and take on a jelly-like texture, and the yolks become creamily greyish-green. Century eggs have been part of Chinese cuisine for ages. It is said to have been discovered by a man in the Hunan province who stumbled upon some eggs that his ducks had laid in a lime pit. They might look unappetising to the uninitiated, but they add an interesting texture to dishes.

NOTES

- Using hot water results in a velvety, smooth texture for the custard. This tip is from Auntie Alicia, who often prepares her steamed eggs simply with eggs, hot water, shallot oil and a drizzle of light soy sauce.
- Straining the egg mixture rids it of any lumps or air bubbles that may impede the smoothness of the dish.
- Steam the egg custard over extremely low heat until it is just set. When you jiggle the bowl of steamed egg, it shouldn't be runny but just have a slight give to it.
- To make this into a more substantial dish, add a layer of seasoned minced pork while whisking up the egg mixture.
- To save on cooking time, use cooked salted duck eggs available from the market, so you can skip having to cook the salted eggs and just peel and chop them up along with the century eggs.

Salted Radish Omelette

Chye Poh Neng

Serves 4–6 as part of a meal

This is the perfect salty, eggy accompaniment to a bowl of soothing, bland rice porridge. All you need are some crunchy pickles on the side and you have yourself one of the most satisfying meals. When I was growing up, rice porridge was always served with these crunchy pickles called *chye sim*, some slices of pan-fried luncheon meat and this dish of salted radish omelette. Somehow, these briny, salty dishes tasted even more delicious tempered with the porridge. Simple, inexpensive and hits the spot.

75 g salted radish (*chye poh*)
3 eggs
½ tsp sugar
1–2 dashes ground white pepper
2 Tbsp neutral-tasting oil
such as canola or sunflower oil

1. Soak the salted radish in water for about 10 minutes to remove some of its saltiness. Drain and squeeze dry.
2. Beat the eggs with the sugar and pepper.
3. Heat the oil in a wok over medium-low heat. Add the salted radish and stir-fry until lightly golden and fragrant. The little bits of radish will begin to jump around in the wok.
4. When this happens, add the beaten eggs and adjust the heat to medium-high. Let cook until the omelette is almost set and the base is golden brown. Flip it over in one deft motion and let the other side take on some colour. This may take another 20–30 seconds.
5. Transfer to a serving plate and serve with rice porridge (page 15).

NOTES

- Use a good quality salted radish (*chye poh*) for this. The kind you're after is the salted variety, not the sweet one. Check that the pack is labelled "salted" rather than "sweet".
- Soak the salted radish for a few minutes to get rid of some of the salt. Be sure not to soak it for too long or it will lose most of its flavour.
- Flipping the omelette in one fell swoop is probably the hardest part of this dish. Make sure the bottom side up is cooked almost 80% through before attempting to flip. The best tool for this is a wide spatula that can support as much of the egg as possible. If you flip too early, you risk ripping the omelette apart. Nothing wrong with that. Practice makes perfect and it'd still taste good, so don't beat yourself up about it should the omelette break.

Whitebait Omelette

Serves 4–6 as part of a meal

These tiny little fish have got a very salty savoury bite to them. They're the small fried things (much tinier than the fried anchovies known as *ikan bilis*) that you can find atop fried rice sometimes. I was at the wet market one day and the stallholder introduced them to me, telling me how these tiny fish taste amazing fried and served with white rice or used in stocks. Intrigued, I bought a box. I've found that crisping them up and cooking them into a golden brown, puffy omelette works beautifully.

75 g whitebait
3 eggs
1 tsp light soy sauce
A dash of ground white pepper
120 ml neutral-tasting oil
such as canola or sunflower oil

1. Rinse the whitebait and drain. Pat dry.
2. Beat the eggs with the light soy sauce and pepper.
3. Heat the oil in a wok over medium-high heat for 1–2 minutes until the oil is very hot. Add the whitebait and fry until they turn light golden brown.
4. Remove from heat and strain the oil and whitebait into a bowl through a sieve. Reserve the oil. Set the whitebait aside to cool and crisp up.
5. Reheat the wok and return about 4 Tbsp oil to the wok. When the oil is very hot, add the eggs, then quickly scatter the fried whitebait over the eggs. The eggs will puff up and bubble around the edges. When it is almost cooked through, flip it over to brown the other side. This should take no more than a minute or so.
6. Transfer to a serving plate and serve with rice.

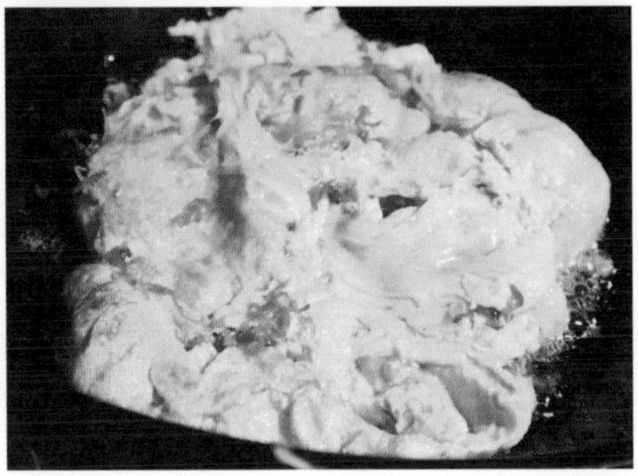

NOTES

- Get fresh, tiny whitebait for this. They come in a larger size as well, but the smaller ones are preferred in this dish.
- Make sure the oil is hot enough before adding the whitebait or they will stick to the bottom of the wok (yes, learn from my mistakes). If that happens, you'll have to clean the wok before attempting the dish again.
- Set the whitebait aside to cool after the initial step of frying. This will allow them to crisp up before they are added to the eggs.

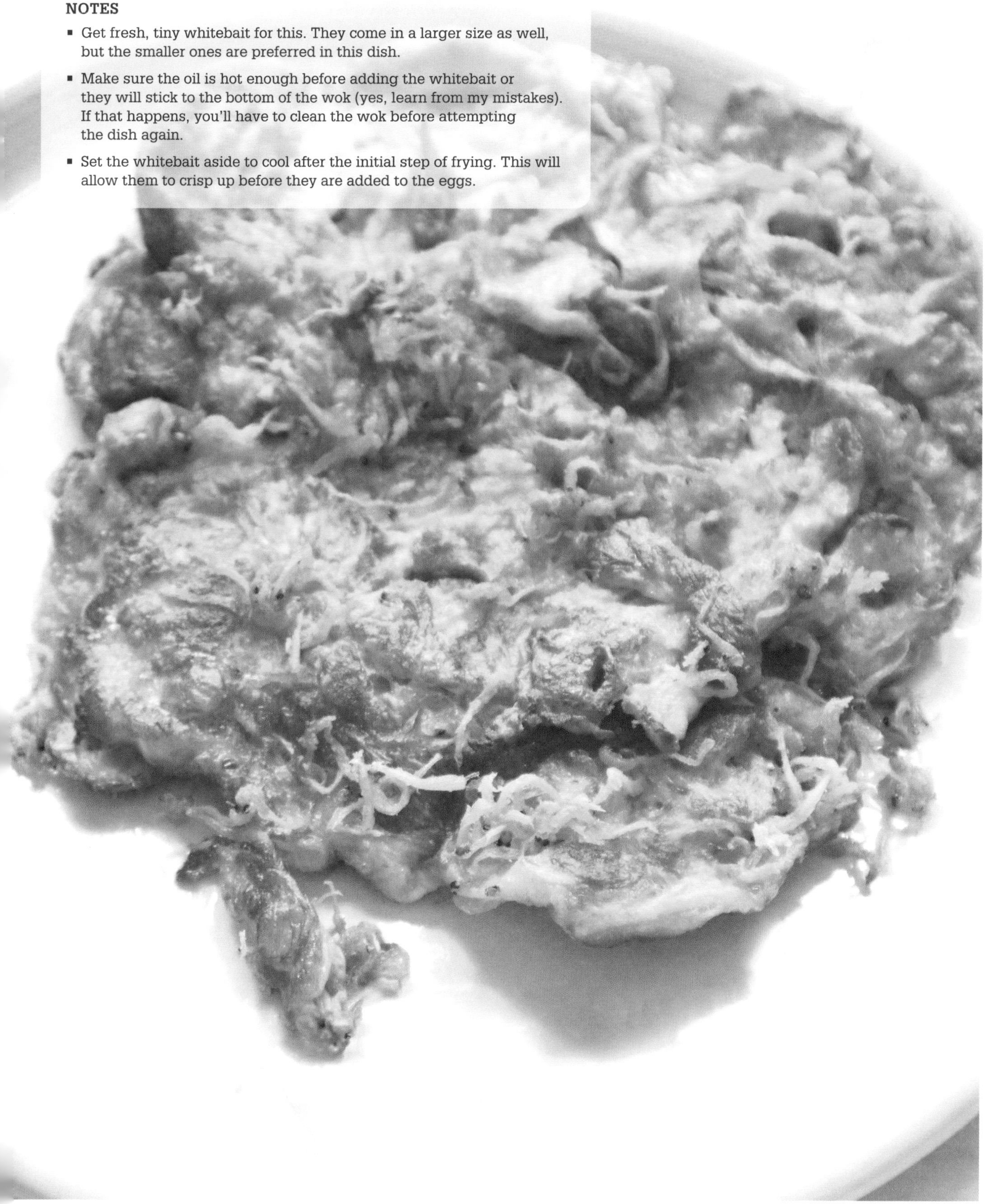

Sunny Side Up

— whatever you want to add a fried egg to

It seems ridiculous that I'm including a recipe for eggs fried sunny side up, but it's really my homage to the humble egg — the everyday protein that many overlook or take for granted, overshadowed by pricier protein options such as fish or chicken.

Have you ever tried just having a well-fried egg atop a bowl of steaming hot white rice, a trickle of soy sauce running down the surface of the egg? My egg-ddicted cousins always request for a fried egg to accompany the rest of the dishes during dinnertime, specifying their preferred doneness for the yolk. The ultimate fried egg, to me, should be crisp and lacily golden around the edges and the bottom. One that you can smell when it's done right, that intense, heightened fragrance of… egg. The yolk should still be runny and the white just cooked, not rubbery. Place piping hot atop rice and drizzle with a condiment of choice for salinity and/or sweetness, then break into the runny yolk and watch it lubricate the rice with its yellow sunshine trail. As they say, everything is made better when you put an egg on it…

Neutral-tasting oil such as canola or sunflower oil
Eggs

1. Heat about 3 Tbsp oil (sufficient for almost deep-frying the egg) in a wok over medium-high heat.
2. When the oil is sufficiently heated, gently crack an egg into the middle of the wok. It will start to bubble and hiss.
3. Cover the wok to allow the top of the egg to cook as the edges fry. This should just take a moment, depending on how well-done you enjoy your yolk. The top should be just-set while the edges golden.
4. Remove the egg from the wok, drizzle with some light soy sauce and serve.

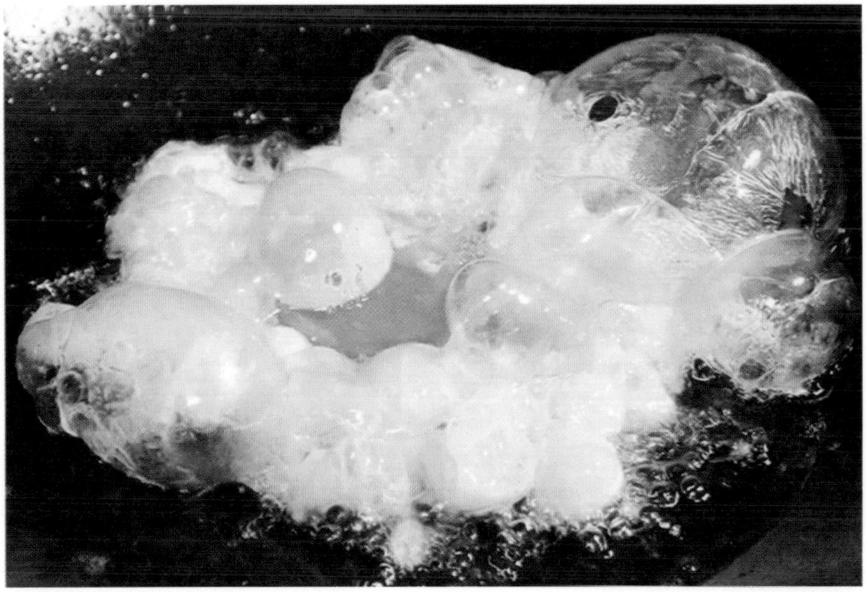

Stir-fried Cabbage with Dried Shrimps

Serves 4–6 as part of a meal

This dish is comfort food at its most soulful, a taste of home when you've been away too long. This familiar, classic combination of sweet, tender cabbage and salty dried shrimps is really a simple dish with just two main ingredients, but it produces something more than the sum of its parts. It is also one of the more crowd-pleasing vegetable dishes and will appeal to young children or greens-averse adults.

1 small round cabbage, 500–600 g
60 g dried shrimps
1 Tbsp neutral-tasting oil such as canola or sunflower oil
½ tsp salt
½ tsp sugar
80–100 ml water
½ tsp light soy sauce

1. Cut the cabbage in half from top to bottom. Cut out and discard the tough inner core at the bottom that resembles a triangle. Lay the cabbage flat-side down, then cut it into big strips about 2-cm wide.
2. Soak the dried shrimps in water for about 20 minutes until softened. Drain well and pound them using a mortar and pestle. You can also choose to chop them with a knife or leave them whole.
3. Heat the oil in a wok over medium-high heat. Add the dried shrimps and stir-fry until the shrimps turn golden brown. Set aside.
4. Crank the heat up to high and add the cabbage chunks. Season with salt and sugar. Use a wok spatula to toss the cabbage around, allowing it to cook down in the wok.
5. Add the water along with the light soy sauce. Return the dried shrimps to the wok. Cover the wok with a lid and let it stew until the cabbage is soft and tender. This may take another 5–8 minutes. Taste and check for seasoning.
6. Dish out and enjoy with rice or rice porridge (page 15).

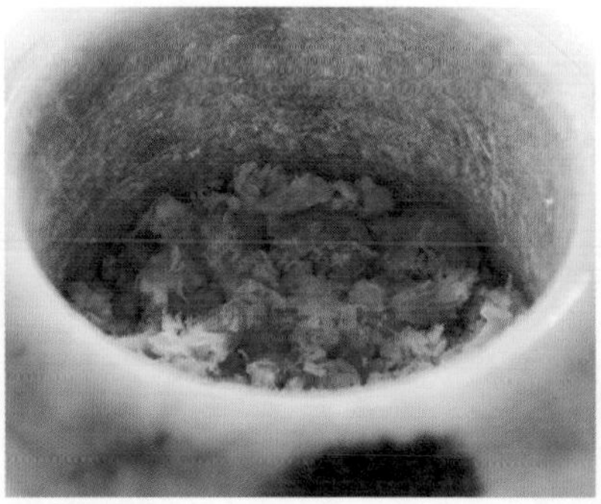

NOTES

- Soaking the dried shrimps will help to soften them before cooking, but take care not to leave them in the water for too long or you may risk all the flavour leeching out.
- I like to pound the dried shrimps to release their flavour into the oil and by extension, into the final dish. Most people leave them whole. This will allow you to bite into the chewy pieces which is quite enjoyable too!

Stir-fried Snow Peas with Baby Corn and Carrot

Serves 4–6 as part of a meal

I remember how I used to prep the veggies with Auntie Alicia for this dish, removing the ends of the snow peas, slicing the carrots (which she cuts into fanciful floral shapes — I don't have the patience or the artistic dexterity for this sort of food art), then soaking the vegetables in water to clean them. The vegetables would be left soaking in bowls of water around the kitchen sink as she preps the other dishes for our meal.

For its lack of an interesting name, this is a vibrant stir-fry with many textures in a single dish. The vegetables are all sweet, crunchy and colourful, and you want them to retain that as much as possible. The dried mushrooms provide a delightful, meaty chew amidst all that crunch. This is a stir-fry that Auntie Alicia cooks very often, occasionally adding in prawns or scallops from the freezer to make the dish more luxurious, so feel free to do so if you have any on hand.

4 dried Chinese mushrooms
150 g snow peas
8–10 spears baby corn
1 medium carrot
2 Tbsp cooking oil or liquid lard (page 16)
3 cloves garlic, peeled and minced
2 Tbsp oyster or abalone sauce

1. Soak the dried Chinese mushrooms in warm water for about 30 minutes or until softened. Squeeze the excess water from the soaked mushrooms. Trim and discard their tough, woody stems. Cut the caps into quarters.
2. Rinse the snow peas and drain. Pinch the stem at the top end of a snow pea and pull downwards to remove the string that runs down the length of the pod. Repeat with all the snow peas. Set aside.
3. Rinse the baby corn and cut each spear into thirds. Set aside.
4. Peel and cut the carrot into 0.5-cm thick rounds.
5. Heat the oil in a wok over medium heat. Lower the heat to low and add the minced garlic. Let fry for a moment, then add the mushrooms and carrot. Turn the heat back up.
6. Add the baby corn and stir-fry for about 2 minutes until the vegetables soften just a little. Add the snow peas and the oyster or abalone sauce, tossing everything together in the wok. Turn off the heat immediately. Taste and adjust the seasoning as needed.
7. Dish out and serve!

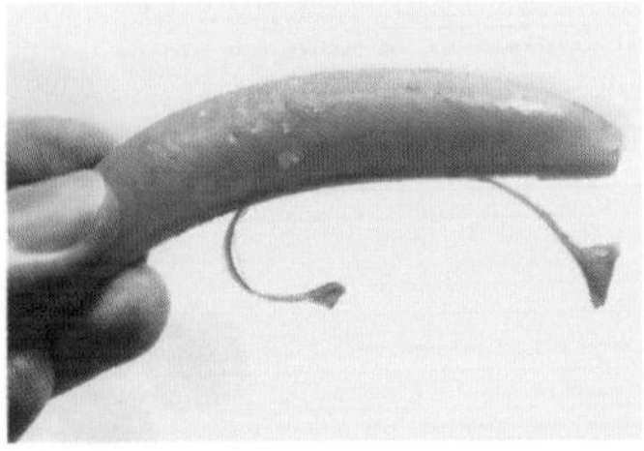
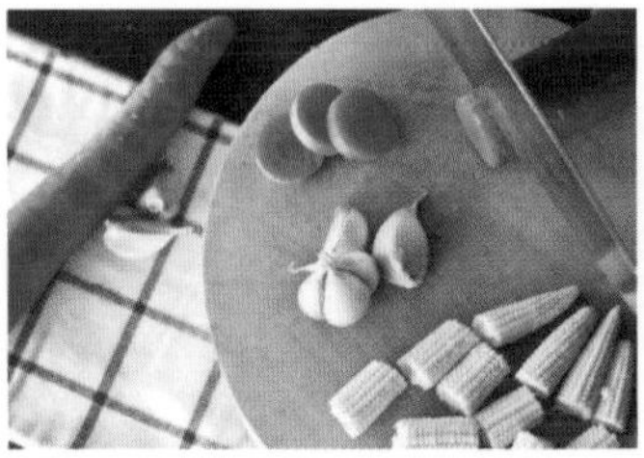

NOTES

- Be careful not to overcook the vegetables! You don't want limp and soggy in this stir-fry. The snow peas cook the quickest, so add them towards the end.
- If adding protein like prawns or scallops, add them midway through cooking to ensure they don't overcook and turn rubbery.
- To take this dish to the next level in terms of fragrance and taste, use liquid lard (page 16) in place of oil.

Stir-fried Bean Sprouts with Salted Fish

Serves 4–6 as part of a meal

A huge plastic bag of bean sprouts freshly purchased from the wet market, plopped on the floor on a lazy weekend morning. The repetitive and therapeutic process of topping and tailing the sprouts, the ends thrown into another plastic bag to be discarded. As a nosy kid with a short attention span, I remember attempting to help Auntie Alicia at times with this task, but I always ended up doing something else, say feeding our family dog with the sprouts instead.

Here, the crunchy bean sprouts are punctuated with the intense saline flavour of crisp-fried salted fish and infused with the aromatic heat from the pounded garlic and chillies. This dish cooks really quickly and the delicate sprouts can go from crunchy to soggy in a matter of seconds, so work fast!

200 g topped and tailed bean sprouts
10 g dried salted fish
2 garlic cloves, peeled
½ red bird's eye chilli
1–2 Tbsp cooking oil or liquid lard (page 16)
½ tsp sugar
½ Tbsp light soy sauce
A handful of coriander leaves

1. Rinse the bean sprouts and drain well.
2. Soak the salted fish in water for about 10 minutes. Drain and cut into small cubes.
3. Mince the garlic and chilli together until fine.
4. Heat the oil or lard in a wok over low heat. Add the salted fish and fry until golden brown. Drain and set aside to cool and crisp up.
5. Without wiping the wok, add the minced garlic and chilli. Cook, allowing the aromas to be released. This should take no more than 20 seconds. Crank the heat up to high and add the bean sprouts, sugar and light soy sauce.
6. Toss for about 20 seconds to cook the bean sprouts lightly. Do this quickly as you want the sprouts to retain some crunch. Remove from heat.
7. Add the fried salted fish cubes and coriander leaves. Transfer to a serving plate. Serve.

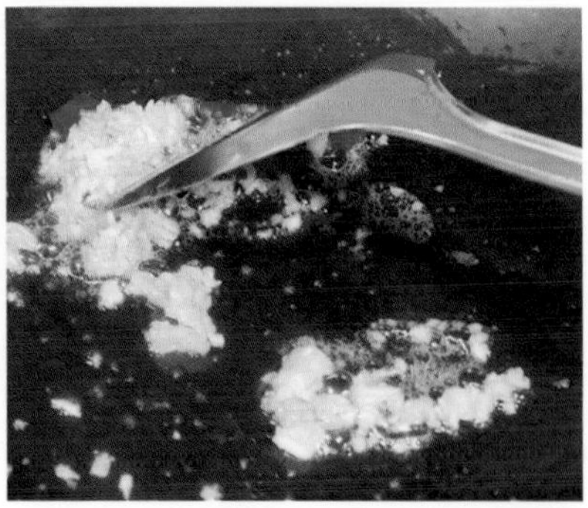

NOTES

- Salted fish is available as hard dried pieces or as slippery slivers cured in jars of brine. When used in cooking, they add a huge flavour boost to the dish. The type typically used in vegetable stir-fries and fried rice is dried salted fish, while salted fish in brine is usually used in cooking clay pot rice or steamed minced meat.
- If you are too lazy to top and tail the bean sprouts yourself, topped and tailed sprouts can be found in some supermarkets. They cost more, but it reduces your prep time. Alternatively, leave the tops and tails on!
- This stir-fry cooks really quickly, so make sure you have everything prepared and ready before starting to cook.

Spicy Long Beans

Serves 4–6 as part of a meal

Like the chilli squid recipe (page 56), this recipe is courtesy of my dad. In fact, it uses the same base chilli sauce as the squid dish — two birds, one stone. He fries up the dried shrimps for the base before adding the chilli sauce and the long beans. The resulting sauce resembles dried shrimp sambal (page 17). Depending on your inclination, you can choose to let the sauce reduce and darken further or allow it to be more moist and vibrant. It's all a matter of personal preference. On this same note, I know soggy vegetables are considered sacrilege in the culinary world and, in most cases, vegetables should be cooked al dente. With this dish however, I unapologetically, unabashedly admit that I love soggy long beans. I cook them until they are almost caramelised, so their limp bodies can take to the sauce even more.

5–6 Tbsp chilli sauce (page 56)
20 g dried shrimps
200 g long beans
80 ml cooking oil
1 Tbsp light soy sauce

1. Prepare the chilli sauce according to the recipe.
2. Soak the dried shrimps in water for about 20 minutes until softened. Drain well, then pound them using a mortar and pestle. Skip this step if you prefer to leave them chunky.
3. Cut the long beans into roughly equal lengths, about 5 cm. The uniform size will help them cook evenly and also be aesthetically pleasing.
4. Heat the oil in a wok over medium heat. Add the dried shrimps and let cook until lightly golden.
5. Add the chilli sauce and let it heat up. Toss in the long beans and stir-fry until the beans are to your desired doneness. This can take 2–5 minutes, depending on your preference. Really, the best way is to take a stalk out and taste.
6. Season with the light soy sauce. Dish out and serve.

NOTES

- You can choose to leave the dried shrimps whole if you prefer to bite into chewable, sizeable chunks. My dad pounds the shrimps up and that's how I usually do it too.
- For al dente long beans, shorten the cooking time accordingly.
- If you prefer the sauce to be drier and darker, allow the chilli sauce to caramelise before tossing in the long beans.
- If you don't want to go through the trouble of cooking your own chilli sauce, use a good quality store-bought one, preferably from a restaurant or hawker stall of your choice.

Lotus Root, Peanut and Pork Rib Soup

Serves 6–8 as part of a meal

A piping hot bowl of this soup, with sweetness from the addition of goodies such as Chinese wolfberries and Chinese red dates, is just the antidote needed to nourish the body and whet the appetite when one is under the weather. In line with the traditional Chinese belief that you are what you eat, soups are typically fed to loved ones to provide an extra boost of nutrition during meals. I remember being fed bowlfuls of hot soups as a kid, the adults always telling my cousins and I to "*he tang*", literally "drink soup", if we wanted gleaming smooth skin and good eyesight. Such was the power of a long, slow boil, extracting all the health benefits from the ingredients. This soup is another one of those iconic dishes that can be found when you sup in someone's home here for dinner — every family has their own way of preparing this homely soup. Here's the way mine does it. This recipe is from Auntie Alicia's many years of cooking. She adds in a mix of dried seafood to impart that intense savouriness to the soup and uses just the right amount of dried raw peanuts to enhance, not overwhelm.

30 g dried octopus
1 slice dried whelk
8 Chinese red dates
1 medium lotus root, about 300 g
500 g pork ribs
4 dried scallops
150 g dried raw peanuts
2 litres water
1 tsp salt
2 Tbsp Chinese wolfberries

1. Start by preparing the dried ingredients. Soak the dried octopus and dried whelk in water for about 15 minutes to allow them to soften slightly. Soak the red dates for about 10 minutes. Drain before using.
2. In a pot, add enough water to submerge the pork ribs and bring to a boil. Add the pork ribs and blanch for about 5 minutes. Drain and rinse the ribs.
3. Wash the lotus root well. Trim and discard the ends, then peel the skin using a vegetable peeler. Slice into rounds roughly about 1-cm thick.
4. Rinse the peanuts and drain.
5. Place the pork ribs, dried octopus, dried whelk, dried scallops, lotus root and peanuts in a large stockpot or clay pot. Add the water and salt. Bring to a boil, then lower the heat and let it simmer for at least 2 hours.
6. Add the red dates and Chinese wolfberries and simmer for another 15 minutes. Taste and adjust the seasoning.
7. Enjoy piping hot!

NOTES

- Using a combination of dried seafood (octopus, whelk and scallops), results in a more flavourful soup as compared to using just one type of dried seafood. The dried octopus can be substituted with dried squid. Experiment and see which you prefer.
- The Chinese wolfberries are added towards the end of cooking to prevent them from being overcooked. This also ensures that they maintain their vibrancy and shape.
- Use the kind of peanuts that are round and tiny, instead of the long, oval ones. The latter is more suited for braising, to serve as an appetiser or to go with porridge or *bak kut teh* (pork rib soup).
- You will need to boil this soup for a minimum of 2 hours. I usually boil it for 3–4 hours. The longer boil not only results in a more flavourful soup, it also ensures that the pork ribs are fork-tender. If not given sufficient time to cook down, the ribs will be stringy and tough.

Old Cucumber Soup

Serves 6–8 as part of a meal

I've been told that this old cucumber soup is highly nutritious, cooling for the body and excellent for the skin. When one is on the verge of getting a sore throat or when the weather is unbearably hot, this is the perfect soup to tame the yang. Steam up some rice, splash some light soy sauce into a tiny saucer with sliced chillies for dipping and you have yourself a meal.

1 dried whelk
8 Chinese red dates
500 g pork ribs
1 old cucumber
6 dried scallops
2 Tbsp Chinese wolfberries
2 litres water
1 tsp salt

1. Soak the dried whelk in water for about 15 minutes to allow it to soften slightly. Soak the red dates for about 10 minutes. Drain before using.
2. In a pot, add enough water to submerge the pork ribs and bring to a boil. Add the pork ribs and blanch for about 5 minutes. Drain and rinse the ribs.
3. Wash and scrub the skin of the old cucumber thoroughly. Cut it lengthwise in half, then scrape out and discard the seeds. Cut the hollowed-out cucumber into large chunks.
4. Place the pork ribs, old cucumber, dried whelk and dried scallops in a large stockpot or clay pot. Add the water and salt. Bring to a boil, then lower the heat, cover with a lid and let it simmer for 2–3 hours.
5. Add the red dates and Chinese wolfberries and simmer for another 15 minutes. Taste and adjust the seasoning.
6. Enjoy piping hot!

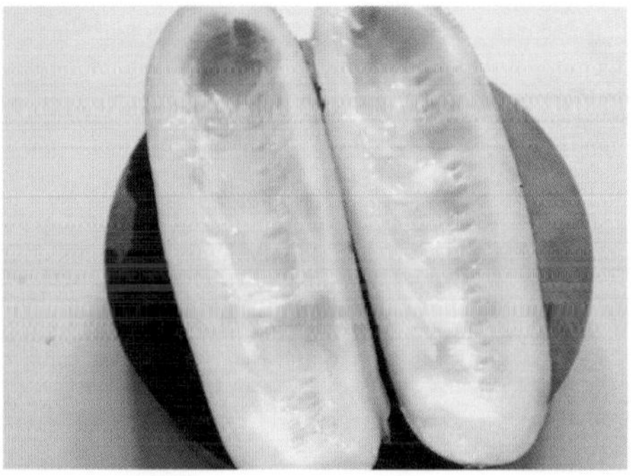

NOTES

- Old cucumbers are cucumbers that have matured and aged, their skins becoming all wrinkly and brown in the process. Leave the skins on when you're making this soup — that's where most of the nutrients are found. The cucumber will also disintegrate into mush without the skin to hold it together. This actually saves on the prep work and makes life easier!
- Blanching the pork ribs helps get rid of any impurities and results in a less cloudy soup. After boiling, wash the ribs thoroughly under running tap water to remove any residue and scum.

Herbal Chicken Soup

Serves 2

Chicken soup for the soul is exactly what this nourishing tonic is. Every family has its own brew using various concoctions of traditional Chinese herbs and chicken, sometimes black, sometimes only the carcass and sometimes thighs. Whatever the permutation, the purpose is always the same — to provide nourishment for members of the family. As you consume the precious liquid, you can almost feel it working its magic, the many health-giving properties of the herbs assimilating every pore of your body. It's hard not to feel good when you're drinking a bowl of home-brewed herbal soup.

This recipe comes from Tiffanie, a good friend of mine. She is a meticulous cook with sky-high standards. Her version of this soup is rich in flavour from the generous use of dried ingredients and herbs, their flavours slowly extracted from the long, gentle simmering time. She tells me that this soup will keep the mind clear and in tip-top condition, while rejuvenating and nourishing the qi in the body.

2 chicken legs (bone-in)
4 dried Chinese mushrooms
4 dried scallops
4 Chinese red dates
1 Tbsp Chinese wolfberries
4 slices Solomon's seal rhizome (*yu zhu*)
2 slices wild Chinese yam (*shan yao*)
2 codonopsis roots (*dang shen*)
2 slices astragalus root (*huang qi*)
6 slices angelica root (*dang gui*)
6 slices lovage (*chuan xiong*)
2 slices licorice root (*gan cao*)
1 litre water

1. For a less oily soup, pull off and discard the skin of the chicken legs before cooking. Rinse well.
2. Boil a pot of water and lightly blanch the chicken to get rid of any impurities. Drain and rinse the chicken. Place in a saucepan or clay pot.
3. Soak the dried ingredients and herbs in water for about 5 minutes, then give them a quick rinse and place in the saucepan or clay pot with the chicken.
4. Add the water and cover the pan or pot with a lid. Simmer over very low heat. The water should barely break into a boil, so do check on the soup occasionally to ensure that it isn't boiling vigorously. Let the soup brew for at least 4 hours. During this time, skim off and discard any foam/impurities that may rise to the surface of the stock from time to time. If you feel the soup is drying up, top up with more water.
5. After 4 hours, the soup will be intensely flavoured, yet clear, and the chicken will be fall-off-the-bone tender with slight browning at the edges. Ladle into bowls and serve hot.

NOTES

- Blanching the chicken helps to seal the meat and prevent impurities from making the soup murky.
- The soup is brewed over low heat for a long period of time (4–6 hours) to ensure clarity of the soup and its flavours. The resulting soup has depth yet maintains a light mouthfeel.

Homemade Chicken Essence

Serves 2–3

Across all cultures, some variant of chicken soup is always touted as a health-giving elixir, to restore, rejuvenate and revive. In addition to chicken soup, the Chinese also have chicken essence, which is pure essence of chicken, slowly extracted over 4–6 hours of double boiling. So potent is it that one shot is deemed sufficient. I remember being given these tiny bottles of store-bought chicken essence, gently heated up, during examination periods, as an assurance against illness.

My friend Kimberly told me how her mother who is Cantonese, would order a mother (or stewing) hen from the nearby wet market and use it to brew this chicken essence. She would even use an old-school double boiler meant just for this purpose. The contraption consists of a steaming plate with tiny holes on which the chicken parts sit, with another plate below to collect all the precious chicken essence that will trickle through the holes as the chicken steams. Not wanting to lug home another piece of kitchen equipment (and annoy my parents with storage issues), I came up with this makeshift version using a ceramic double boiling jar. You can just as easily fashion your own with a steamer.

1 mother (stewing) hen or kampong/ free range chicken
Water, as needed

1. Cut off the head and neck of the chicken and trim the tips of the claws from the feet. Chop the chicken into 8–10 pieces. Alternatively, get the butcher to do this for you.
2. Place an overturned soup bowl into the base of the double boiling jar. (Use a bowl that is slightly smaller than the jar.) Arrange the pieces of chicken around the bowl. Cover the jar with the recessed lid and outer lid and place into a deep pot. Fill the deep pot with water to come halfway up the side of the double boiling jar.
3. Let boil over low heat for 6 hours. Top with more water as necessary. Leave to cool completely before opening the pot and the jar.
4. Remove the spent chicken pieces and set them aside. All the essence would have pooled under the bowl nicely. I think the bowl acts as a suction device. Remove the bowl and watch the golden liquid gush out. Pass it through a sieve into another bowl to ensure clarity.
5. Let the essence sit overnight in the fridge. The following day, skim off the layer of fat and gently re-heat by steaming before serving.

NOTES

- An older bird like a mother/stewing hen has more flavour and makes the essence more intense. If you can't get hold of one, use a free range or kampong chicken.
- After refrigerating, the essence will become jelly-like from all the collagen, with a layer of fat on top. Skim the fat off before serving.

“Among all peoples and in all times,
every significant event in life — be it wedding,
triumph, or birth — is marked by a meal or the sharing
of food or drink. The meal is the emblem of civilisation.
What would one know of life as it should be lived
or nights as they should be spent apart from meals?”

~ James & Kay Salter

Special Occasions

The dishes in this section are ones that often grace my family's dinner table during special occasions. Much like a child leaping into a parent's warm embrace after falling down, these are comforting patterns we know we can always rely on. Like many Chinese families, the most important festival that we celebrate is the Lunar New Year, an extravaganza of feasting and visiting that goes on for several days.

On the eve, lunch for us would always be steamboat at my maternal grandma's place. There would be a metal hotpot in the middle of the table filled with an intensely brewed chicken stock and dishes piled high with raw sliced pork, fish, prawns, a variety of processed seafood balls, as well as an array of fresh vegetables. By the end of the meal, the stock, having been flavoured by all of these ingredients, becomes even more sumptuous. My grandma's wooden table may be humble, but she takes great pride in the preparation and selection of each ingredient, and it tastes and looks better than anything you'll find in a fancy hotpot spot.

The main snack star of the show every Lunar New Year would be my dad's pineapple tarts. He doesn't cook often, but when he does, everything he touches is gold. The pineapple filling for his pineapple tarts is always hand-grated and cooked over the stove for several hours, the constant stirring non-negotiable as the water evaporates, concentrating the flavours and sugars. It's not an easy arm workout, not to mention the blisters that appear from the hours of constant stirring with a wooden spoon. When baked, the house smells of buttery pastry and sweet heat. The aroma of tender, fragrant dough encasing pineapple jam hits your olfactory senses even before you bite into the tart, the whiff of butter getting into the back of your nostrils.

For dinner, we'd adjourn to my paternal side, where my uncle's home would always welcome us with a huge dinner feast, all painstakingly prepared by Auntie Alicia. There would be freshly-caught seafood that my uncle would have lugged back from Malaysia. Superbly fresh fish, steamed simply with ginger and sour plums, and sea prawns fried with a sweet and sour sauce or baked with butter and garlic.

There would also be my grandpa's roast pork belly, sliced into little chunks for easy picking, the skin intensely burnished and giving off a loud crackling sound with every bite. Any leftovers would be added to stews in the following days, luxuriantly paired with collagen-rich goodies like sea cucumber and fish maw, the resultant sauce draping itself around these prized Chinese delicacies. After having our fill at dinner, we would head back home and await the visiting frenzy that would ensue the following day.

Five-spice Meat Rolls

Ngoh Hiong

Makes 10–12 rolls

Every Lunar New Year, this would be the most highly-anticipated dish on my grandma's lunch table, where a huge feast would beckon and welcome us all on the very first day. She is renowned for these golden fritters, fried till the bean curd skin shatters into crisp, saline shards in your mouth, giving way to a generous filling that's been lightly spiced with its namesake. She's been making these for decades and every single time, they come out perfectly seasoned, all based on her very attuned instincts in the kitchen. Her *ngoh hiong* has a good amount of refreshing crunch from water chestnuts, patiently peeled and chopped into little cubes for her signature dish.

If you're cooking for a large group or party, feel free to double the recipe. That would necessitate a fair bit of chopping, but you make a good amount of rolls and any leftovers can be stashed in the freezer to be fried up whenever you fancy. I find when there's nothing on my schedule, the repetitive, mindless chopping of the water chestnuts is almost therapeutic.

3 shallots
8 water chestnuts
60 g carrot
3 cream crackers
160 g peeled prawns
250 g minced pork belly or shoulder
2 tsp ground white pepper
1 Tbsp five-spice powder
1 Tbsp sesame oil
1 Tbsp light soy sauce
Dried bean curd skin, as needed

1. Prepare the ingredients. Peel the shallots and chop them up finely. Peel the water chestnuts and cut into little cubes. Peel the carrot and grate finely using a box grater. Crush the cream crackers. Mince the prawns until they are almost paste-like.
2. In a big bowl, combine the prawns, pork, shallots, water chestnuts, carrot, cream crackers, pepper, five-spice powder, sesame oil and light soy sauce. Mix the entire mass until it comes together. I find it easiest to use my hands to press the mixture together while mixing. Set aside.
3. Prepare the bean curd skin. They come in large rectangular sheets. There will be natural fold lines, so use that as a guide to cut them into smaller sheets. For this recipe, the skin is cut roughly into 22 x 13-cm rectangles. Wipe the bean curd sheets briefly with a clean, damp cloth to remove any excess salt. Prepare a small bowl or cup of water.
4. Place a sheet of bean curd skin on the table with the shorter side facing you. Spoon about 2 Tbsp filling across the length of the shorter side. Fold the two longer sides of the bean curd skin over the filling and roll it up tightly. Use a bit of water to dampen and seal the edges. Repeat until the ingredients are used up.
5. Arrange the rolls on a steaming plate and steam for 5–8 minutes. You can then freeze or refrigerate the steamed rolls if you're doing this in advance. If frying immediately, let the rolls cool and pat the surface dry with paper towels.
6. Heat sufficient oil in a wok over medium heat and deep-fry the rolls until they turn golden brown. Drain well. Alternatively, use a deep-fryer or an air-fryer.

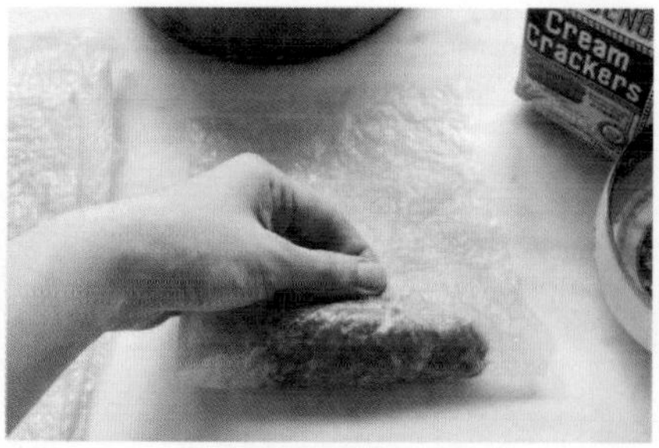

NOTES

- Five-spice powder is also known as *ngoh hiong hoon* in Hokkien. It is typically a blend of cassia, star anise, fennel seeds, cloves and Szechuan pepper. Depending on the brand you get, there could be a couple of extra spices added on top of the five main staples. This spice pairs really well with fatty meats and roasts. You can find packets of these sold in Chinese medicinal halls. The spices constituting the blend are also believed to have healing properties, highlighting the Chinese belief in food as medicine.
- The dried bean curd skin is incredibly salty. Wipe off some of the excess salt with a clean damp cloth before filling the rolls.
- When we were young, my grandma would hand mince the meat for these rolls with a cleaver. If you wish to, you could purchase a slab of pork and do the same. She has since resorted to purchasing ready minced pork to save on the heavy duty work.

Teochew Braised Vegetables

Chap Chye

Serves 6–8 generously as part of a meal

I didn't grow up eating *chap chye*, at least not until Auntie Alicia learnt to prepare this from a neighbour's grandmother, who was Teochew. It was such a huge hit that it has since been welcome into our family with open arms. And it is no mere occasional house visitor. It has in fact been designated an honorary status as a mainstay on our table for reunion meals.

The Chinese love foods for their texture and ability to soak up whatever they are flavoured with. This dish embodies just that with the amalgamation of all these textures that make each mouthful so thrilling: the fine strands of black hair moss (*fatt choy*), chewy dried Chinese mushrooms and mock abalone meat, crunchy black fungus, the slight bite of the dried lily bud and chunks of cabbage and button mushrooms, all bound together by a flavourful, umami-packed sauce with the addition of fermented bean curd (*lam yee*).

1.5 kg napa cabbage
30 g dried lily buds
35 g dried black fungus
15 g black hair moss (*fatt choy*)
10 dried Chinese mushrooms
2 cans button mushrooms (198 g net weight for each can)
1 can baby corn (200 g net weight)
130 g fermented bean curd (*lam yee*)
3 Tbsp canola oil
4 cans mock abalone meat (285 g net weight for each can)
2 Tbsp abalone sauce, oyster sauce or fermented soy bean paste (*tau cheo*)
1/2 tsp salt

1. Cut the cabbage in half from top to bottom. Lay it flat-side down and cut each half into chunks.
2. Soak the dried lily buds, black fungus and black hair moss separately in water for 15–20 minutes until softened. Tie each lily bud into a knot. Cut the black fungus into smaller pieces. Discard any hard bits.
3. Soak the dried Chinese mushrooms in warm water for about 30 minutes or until softened. Squeeze excess water from the soaked mushrooms. Trim and discard the stems, then cut the caps into large chunks.
4. Open the cans of button mushrooms and baby corn. Drain and rinse lightly. Cut the baby corn into thirds.
5. Drain the fermented bean curd from its brine. Mash it with a fork until broken up into tiny, crumbly bits.
6. Preheat a large stockpot over high heat. When sufficiently heated, lower the heat and add the oil. Add the mashed fermented bean curd and fry for about 3 minutes until its fragrance is released and it takes on some colour.
7. Add the cabbage in 3 batches, allowing each batch to reduce first to make space before adding the subsequent batch. It will seem as though there isn't enough space to cook all that cabbage, but trust me, it will reduce a fair bit.
8. When all the cabbage has been added and combined in the pot, add the dried mushrooms, black fungus, lily buds and button mushrooms.
9. Open the cans of mock abalone and add juices and all to the pot. Top all the 4 cans with water and add that to the pot to form the base of your stew.
10. Add the black hair moss and baby corn. Be sure to separate the hair moss into smaller clumps with your fingers as you add them to the pot.
11. Add the abalone sauce, oyster sauce or fermented soy beans and the salt. Let it cook for another 15 minutes, until the cabbage is soft and the dish comes together.
12. Consume heartily or let rest overnight for the flavours to mingle and come together.

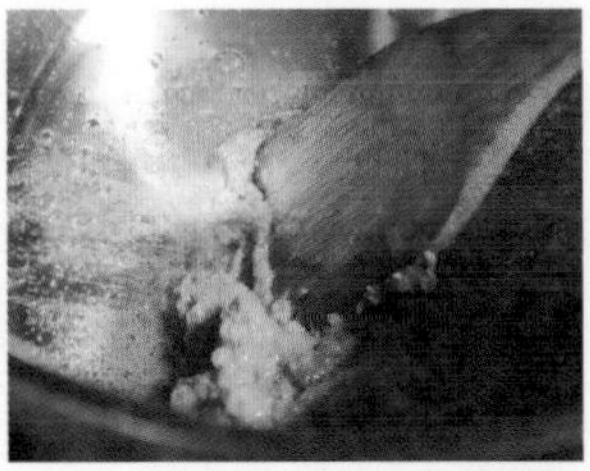
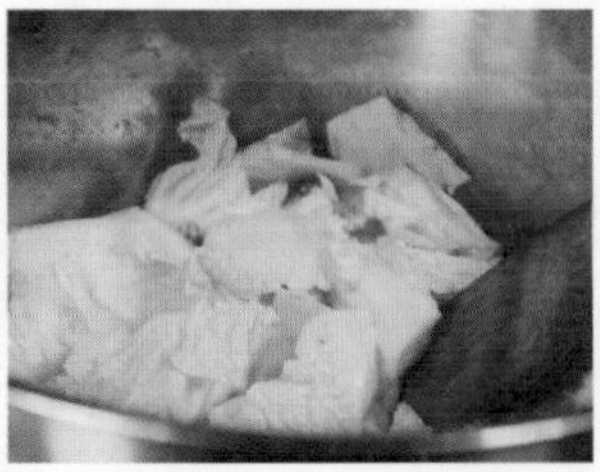

NOTES

- The Peranakans use fermented soy beans in their version. This is the Teochew style which relies on fermented bean curd for seasoning.
- Fermented bean curd is one of the key ingredients of this dish, adding richness to the sauce. Think of it as Chinese cheese that adds that extra oomph or X-factor to a dish. As with many things delicious, it is the product of time and the process of fermentation. Cubes of firm tofu are first fermented, then soaked in brine, resulting in this creamy, cheesy, funky concoction so iconic in Chinese cuisine. Some have got red rice yeast added to it, imbuing it with that rose-tinted hue.
- There is no use of garlic, chives or onions in this dish, making it completely "*chay*", perfect for the most devout of vegetarians to consume. To make it vegan, omit the abalone or oyster sauce and add some fermented soy beans (*tau cheo*) in its place.

Steamed Radish Cake

Lor Bak Gou

Makes two 23 x 7-cm cakes

Every year, on the first day of the Lunar New Year, we would start out visiting my uncle in the morning, where there would be a plethora of snacks prepared by Auntie Alicia. The living room table would be filled with tubs of our favourite festive goodies. There would be wafer-thin love letters, melt-in-your-mouth almond cookies, melon seeds, tubs of my dad's home-made pineapple tarts and squares of smoky-sweet, chewy barbecued meat (*bak kwa*), all for the taking. Without fail, there would be aluminium trays of radish cake, freshly steamed and adorned with all the trimmings — deep-fried shallots for flavour and crunch, chopped spring onions for a hint of green freshness and slices of vibrantly red bird's eye chillies for those who dare. Auntie Alicia makes this radish cake with a generous amount of shredded white radish and tons of umami-rich components like dried scallops, dried shrimps and dried Chinese mushrooms, which lend remarkable flavour to the finished product. It does involve some prep work, so you can choose to prepare the batter the night before and steam it just before serving.

40 g dried shrimps
35 g dried scallops
35 g dried Chinese mushrooms
700 g white radish
100 g pork belly
80 ml cooking oil

Batter
1 litre water, pork stock or a mixture of stock and water
300 g rice flour
1 Tbsp tapioca starch
1½ tsp sugar
1½ tsp salt
2 tsp light soy sauce
A dash of ground white pepper

Garnish
Chopped spring onions
Fried shallots (page 16)
Sliced red chillies

1. Soak the dried shrimps and scallops separately in water for about 20 minutes until softened. Drain well. Pound them separately using a mortar and pestle until fine.
2. Soak the dried Chinese mushrooms in warm water for about 30 minutes or until softened. Squeeze excess water from the soaked mushrooms. Trim and discard the stems, then slice the caps into small squares.
3. Peel the radish using a vegetable peeler, then grate coarsely using a grater.
4. Slice the pork belly into thin slices across the grain.
5. Prepare the batter. In a measuring jug or big bowl, whisk the water/stock, rice flour, tapioca starch, sugar, salt, light soy sauce and pepper together. Set the batter aside.
6. Heat the oil in a wok over medium heat. When the oil is hot, reduce the heat to low and add the pounded dried shrimps. Fry for a few minutes until the dried shrimps start to foam. Add the dried scallops and fry for another few minutes until lightly golden.
7. Add the mushrooms and pork belly and cook until the pork starts to take on some colour and is lightly cooked. Add the grated radish and stir-fry for a minute to lightly cook.
8. Add the batter gradually, stirring as you go, to mix everything well. The mixture will slowly thicken. At this point, turn off the heat. Taste and adjust the seasoning if necessary.
9. Pour the mixture equally into 2 aluminium loaf tins (each about 23 x 7-cm). Place in a steamer and steam over medium-high heat for 20–25 minutes or until a wooden skewer inserted into the middle of the cakes comes out clean.
10. Set aside to cool a little before cutting to serve. To serve, cut the cakes into large cubes and top with chopped spring onions, fried shallots and sliced red chillies.

NOTES

- Ensure the dried seafood and mushrooms are cut into tiny, tiny pieces, to enable the flavours to meld with the radish cake.
- The pork belly can be substituted with Chinese sausages (*lup cheong*).
- Cooking the liquid batter to a thick viscosity prior to steaming will ensure that the radish cake cooks to the correct texture.

Braised Pork Belly Buns

Kong Bak Pau

Serves 4–6

Way before these little parcels of steamed, fluffy white buns imploded onto the culinary scene, trendily morphing into popular Asian burgers of sorts and housing a wide variety of fillings, there was this — the OG *kong bak pau*. There are many fabulous, famous renditions of pork belly buns around the world, some piled with several crunchy adornments, the pork sourced from a special breed of hog and the bun spread with a unique concoction of umami-packed sauces, but sometimes, simplicity is all you need. A sweet, fluffy steamed bun stuffed with a meltingly tender pork belly braise. The only condiment you need is the glossy dark and sticky braising sauce. Honestly, my favourite part of this dish is dunking the steamed bun in an obscene amount of the sauce.

1 kg pork belly, thickly sliced
6 dried Chinese mushrooms
350 ml water
6 garlic cloves, left whole with skin on
12–14 Chinese steamed buns

Marinade
1 star anise
1 cinnamon stick
½ tsp five-spice powder
5 Tbsp dark soy sauce
1 Tbsp oyster sauce
1 Tbsp light soy sauce
½ tsp salt
1 Tbsp sesame oil
A good dash of ground white pepper

1. Combine the ingredients for the marinade and add the pork belly. Mix well, cover and leave to marinate overnight or at least for a few hours.
2. Soak the dried Chinese mushrooms in warm water for about 30 minutes or until softened. Squeeze excess water from the soaked mushrooms and reserve the soaking liquid. Trim and discard the stems of the mushrooms. Leave the caps whole or halve them if they are big.
3. Empty the marinated pork with its marinade into a stewing pot. Add about 100 ml of the mushroom soaking liquid, the water and the mushrooms and let it stew over low heat. Add the garlic cloves after 30 minutes.
4. The total cooking time will vary, about 1–1½ hours. Top up with more water if the sauce starts to dry up. You'll know when it's done. The meat will be tender and falling apart, and the liquid will be reduced to a flavourful, thick sauce, covering about half the contents of the pot.
5. Skim off any fat or scum that would have risen to the top. Taste and adjust the seasoning to account for any evaporation or addition of more liquid.
6. To serve, steam the buns until soft and hot, then sandwich with one or two chunks of pork belly and drizzle that sauce all over.

NOTES

- When slicing the pork belly, cut them thickly as they will cook down and thin slices won't have quite the same juicy mouthfeel.
- If you prefer the stewed meat to be more on the saucy side, up the amount of liquid in the dish. Just be sure to taste and adjust the seasoning at the end.
- My grandma often made this with a leaner cut of pork such as the shoulder which my uncle prefers. It is less fatty and has its own appeal as well, so if you're squeamish about having too much fat in your dish, try using pork shoulder.

Porridge Kueh

Serves 2

This is an incredibly rare dish to find in Singapore these days and like many of the most amazing dishes around the world, this was borne out of necessity and from not wanting to let anything go to waste in leaner times. Back then, using leftover scraps from cuts of undesired meat, whipping up something to eat with the odds and ends that the rich people snubbed was like transforming lead into gold. In this recipe, leftover rice porridge is turned into a brand new dish, stretching it into sustenance for the coolies in the past. This is a Hokkien dish taught to my grandma by her mother-in-law — do give this dish of our culinary past a try, it is beguiling and the chewiness is absolutely addictive.

40 g dried shrimps
2 garlic cloves, peeled
1 red bird's eye chilli
2–3 Tbsp cooking oil
100 ml water
1 Tbsp light soy sauce
A handful of bean sprouts
A handful of coriander leaves

Dough
150 g rice porridge (make sure it is thick and not too watery)
160–200 g tapioca starch

1. Prepare the dough. Combine the porridge and tapioca starch in a bowl and knead until a smooth dough forms. The amount of flour needed will depend on how watery the porridge is. Start with a little tapioca starch and add more as you go along. The end product should be slightly tacky but easy to work with.
2. Start a pot of water boiling. When the dough is smooth, pinch rounds of it and form into flat sheets. Drop the dough sheets into the boiling water to cook in batches. They are done when they turn opaque white and float. Drain and set aside.
3. Cover the cooked dough with cling wrap and let sit in the refrigerator overnight, or for at least a couple of hours. This will allow them to be sliced more easily.
4. When ready to cook, soak the dried shrimps in water for about 20 minutes until softened. Drain well, then pound them using a mortar and pestle until fine. Add the garlic and chilli and pound into a paste.
5. Take the sheets of dough out of the fridge and slice them into strips. You can slice them thick or thin according to your preference. I usually slice them into strips that resemble thick French fries.
6. Heat the oil in a wok over medium-high heat. Add the dried shrimp, garlic and chilli paste and fry for a few minutes until lightly golden. Add the porridge strips and coat well with the paste.
7. Add the water and light soy sauce, then cover the wok and let the strips cook for 1–2 minutes.
8. Remove the cover and toss in the bean sprouts and coriander leaves. Turn off the heat. The vegetables will cook lightly in the residual heat. Taste and adjust the seasoning as necessary. Dish out and enjoy!

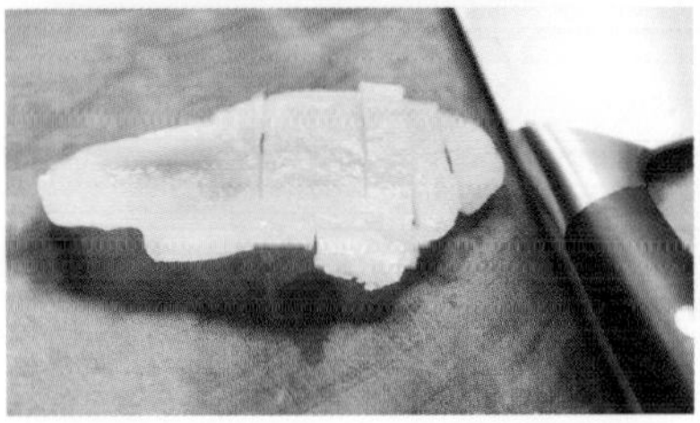

NOTES

- It is easier to start with rice porridge that is almost dried up, with as little liquid content in it as possible.
- Due to the varying moisture content of the porridge and the humidity of the environment, you could need more or less starch than stated in the recipe. Start with the lower amount and gradually increase it until a smooth, slightly tacky dough starts to come together. It should feel easy to work with.
- After the strips of porridge *kueh* are boiled, letting them rest in the refrigerator for at least a few hours (my grandma usually leaves it overnight) will allow them to cool and solidify, making for much neater and easier slicing for the final fry.

Glutinous Rice

Serves 6–8

My grandma's glutinous rice is a feast in itself with its multitude of toppings. The lady didn't go to culinary school nor does she dine in fancy restaurants, but she sure knows a thing or two about elevating dishes. Her glutinous rice is always perfectly steamed and seasoned, imbued with the aromatic flavours of dried shrimps and mushrooms. Depending on her mood, she sometimes prepares shards of fried ginger, fried shallots and slices of darkened, pan-seared pork belly, which she would generously scatter over the steamed rice. She prepares a large amount of these trimmings for our eating pleasure, the textural contrast they provide takes the plate of sticky rice from good to sublime.

350 g white glutinous rice
75 g dried shrimps
10 dried Chinese mushrooms
150 g pork belly
80 ml neutral-tasting oil such as canola or sunflower oil
1 Tbsp sesame oil
1½ Tbsp dark soy sauce
1 Tbsp light soy sauce
1 tsp fish sauce
1 tsp salt
½ tsp sugar
Fried shallots (page 16) and/or fried ginger strips (see Notes)

1. Soak the glutinous rice in water for at least a few hours, or overnight. Drain well before using.
2. Soak the dried shrimps in water for about 15 minutes until softened. Drain well.
3. Soak the dried Chinese mushrooms in warm water for about 30 minutes or until softened. Squeeze excess water from the soaked mushrooms and reserve 200 ml of the soaking liquid. Trim and discard the stems of the mushrooms and slice the caps into chunks.
4. Slice the pork belly into thin strips.
5. Heat the oil in a wok over medium-high heat. When the oil is hot, lower the heat to medium and add the dried shrimps. Fry until the shrimps turn a toasty, bronzed colour. Toss in the mushrooms and add the sesame oil. Stir-fry until fragrant. Remove and set the mixture aside.
6. In the same wok, sear the pork belly. Add 1 Tbsp dark soy sauce and lower the heat to a minimum. Add the drained, pre-soaked glutinous rice, dried shrimp mixture, remaining seasoning and mushroom soaking liquid. Mix well and let the rice absorb the liquid seasoning. Turn off the heat. Taste and adjust the seasoning. If you prefer it saltier, add a splash of light soy sauce.
7. Take a wide, shallow, steaming plate and spoon the rice on it. Place in a steamer. Drizzle a few tablespoonfuls of water over the rice and let it steam over medium-high heat for about 45 minutes or until the rice is cooked through, sticky and tender During the steaming process, give the rice a good toss and turn about twice to ensure the mass is cooked evenly.
8. Transfer to a serving plate and garnish with fried shallots and/or fried ginger before serving.

NOTES

- Glutinous rice is usually served during the Lunar New Year as a symbol of unity and sticking together.
- It is essential to soak the glutinous rice for at least a few hours, or preferably overnight, to allow for easier cooking and for the rice to cook up sticky and soft. I usually measure the rice and leave it to soak overnight on the kitchen countertop, covered with cling wrap.
- You could also steam the pork belly together with the rice instead of stir-frying it.
- To make the fried ginger topping, peel the skin off a good chunk of ginger. Either mince into tiny, fine shreds or pound into shreds using a mortar and pestle. Heat up sufficient oil to cover the ginger in a wok over medium-low heat. Add the ginger and cook until light golden brown. Strain and let cool to crisp up before using.

“This is the kind of food I had fallen in love with:
not trendy, souped-up fantasies,
just something very good to eat.”

~ Julia Child

Sweets

Many traditional desserts come in the form of soups, also known as *tong sui* which literally translates to sugar water, and are purported to have healing qualities. This ties in with the deep-seated Chinese belief that "you are what you eat", treating food as more than mere sustenance and seeking some form of equilibrium within oneself with our diet. When the days are chilly or when one is down with a cold, yang foods like ginger are consumed, to give the body heat and to restore the yin-yang balance. These ingredients and herbs are commonly incorporated into our meals for their restorative properties; nuggets of wisdom and dietary advice passed down from the older generations.

The sweet treats featured here are eaten more as snacks as opposed to dessert at the end of a meal. As a family, we would usually have a platter of freshly cut fruits around the living room table to share after dinner, this doubling up as our something sweet. Traditionally, the Chinese are not big on overly sweet treats and most of our traditional sweets are light in texture and sweetened just so, to whet the appetite instead of inducing a shot of diabetic saccharinity.

Green Bean Soup

Serves 6

A few pandan leaves removed from the pandan plant outside our house. Clear water rushing down against the dried beans with a crinkle of salt. The sound of dried green beans poured into a pot and water sloshing around. Soon, a pot of green bean soup would be ready for the entire family. On hot days, my grandma and Auntie Alicia would rustle up a batch of cooling green bean soup or barley water. The pot of soup would bubble away on the stovetop, the familiar fragrance of the pandan leaves, enlivened by the heat, would waft through the entire house on those lazy afternoons. It is wisdom passed down from the Chinese kitchens that green beans help counteract heatiness in one's body, helping to cool it down internally. The soup is sweetened just so with rock sugar (also believed to have cooling properties) and cooked until the beans have split open, taking on a creamy texture, while the soup develops an attractive, starchy gleam.

300 g dried green beans
1 Tbsp coarse salt
10 g pandan leaves
1.5 litres water
90 g rock sugar or to taste
15 g sago

1. To rinse the beans, place them in a basin with the salt. Fill the basin with water and scrub the beans with your hands, draining and refilling the water while repeating the scrubbing motion. The salt aids in the removal of any dirt and grit on the beans. Do this about 4 times until the water runs clear. Drain well.
2. Wash the pandan leaves and wipe them dry. Tie them into a knot.
3. Place the beans, 1.5 litres water and pandan leaves in a pot or slow cooker. Let it come to a boil, then lower the heat and simmer for 35–45 minutes or until the beans have split and opened up.
4. Add the rock sugar and stir to help it dissolve.
5. Rinse the sago and drain well. Add to the pot of soup and let cook for 5–10 minutes until the sago becomes transparent.
6. Ladle into bowls and enjoy the soup piping hot. Store any leftovers in the fridge to be enjoyed cold the following day.

NOTES

- Washing the beans with coarse grains of salt helps to remove any grit or dirt on the surface of the beans. To do this, place the green beans, salt and some water in a pot. Scrub and rub the beans in this salted water.
- The sago is essential to the final texture of the dish, thickening it with its starchiness. However, the longer the sago sits in the soup, the more water it will absorb, resulting in the soup becoming thick. If this happens, dilute the entire mass with more water until it reaches your desired consistency again.
- You could also add a small slice of aged tangerine peel to the pot. This aged peel is intense in flavour, so a tiny bit will add sufficient citrusy spritz to your dish.

Lotus Seed and White Fungus Dessert

Cheng Tng

Serves 4

Every Lunar New Year, this is the something sweet (*tian*) that's always doled out on our table, a symbol of good luck for the months. During house visits, we would all be given bowlfuls of this sweet, clear soup afloat with goodies like sweet red dates, yellow gingko nuts the shape of a celestial beauty's eyes and plumped-up dried longans. The kids would always be reminded to consume more gingko nuts for their memory-boosting properties, perfect for retaining information for the year's examinations. This is probably one of the healthiest desserts you'll ever come across.

Although the soup is usually consumed hot, any leftovers can be chilled for consumption the following day. The recipe below is based on the one my maternal grandma makes for us and she whips up a phenomenal *cheng tng*. Everything is prepared from scratch, no shortcuts taken, and you can taste it in the final product. She takes time to soften the lotus seeds, shells the gingko nuts, removes their paper-thin skins and the bitter shoot in the middle, then cooks them in a sugar syrup. A real labour of love considering the vast amount she prepares for the entire extended family during the Lunar New Year.

50 g lotus seeds
Water, as needed
30 g dried white fungus
40 g dried longans
4–5 pandan leaves
8 Chinese red dates
60 g light brown sugar or rock sugar, to taste

Gingko Nuts
30 dried gingko nuts
250 ml water
40 g light brown sugar or rock sugar

1. The lotus seeds will take time to softened and cook. Start by soaking them in hot water for about an hour or longer if you have the time to spare. Fill a pot with 600 ml water. Bring to a boil and add the lotus seeds. Cover and simmer for about 15 minutes until the lotus seeds are soft.
2. Soak the white fungus in water for about 20 minutes to soften. Tear the white fungus up into smaller pieces, discarding the tough inner core.
3. Soak the dried longans in water for about 15 minutes until softened.
4. Wash the pandan leaves and wipe them dry. Tie them into a knot.
5. If using dried gingko nuts, pound the shells with a small hammer to remove the shells. Boil the gingko nuts for about 5 minutes, then drain and rinse, removing any remaining skin from each one. Using a toothpick or wooden skewer, pierce the middle of each gingko nut, removing the bitter pith inside.
6. Combine the gingko nuts, 250 ml water and sugar in a small pot, boiling it together for about 10 minutes.
7. Add the dried longans, white fungus, red dates, pandan leaves and sugar to the pot with the lotus seeds. Top up with more water until the ingredients are just submerged. Add the gingko nuts along with its liquid. Let the entire mass simmer for about 15 minutes. Adjust the level of sweetness to taste.
8. Ladle into bowls and enjoy!

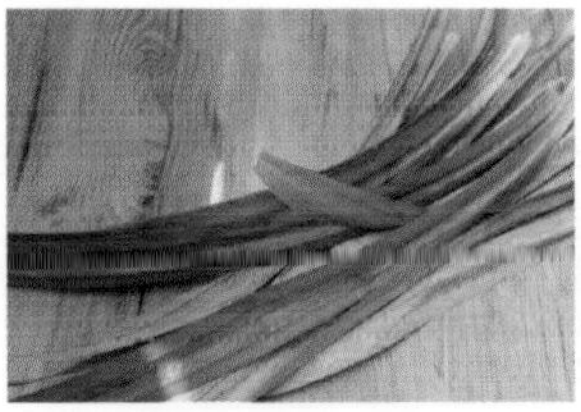

NOTES

- The commercially packed gingko nuts found in the supermarket don't taste quite the same as these. If you're going through all the trouble to make *cheng tng*, you might as well get all the components right. As of the date of this writing, I have not come across a packaged brand that I would gladly consume!
- Soaking the lotus seeds in hot water before cooking reduces its overall cooking time. Otherwise, they take an eternity to go from hard to melding.
- Cooking the gingko nuts with the sugar syrup is key to this dish. This process imparts an initial layer of flavour to the gingko nuts before the eventual commingling of all components to result in *cheng tng* soup.
- If you have a pressure cooker, you could dump all the ingredients inside and let the cooker extract all the goodness from the goodies in as short a time as possible. My grandma has since taken to this method after being gifted with one!

Snow Fungus and Pear Soup

Serves 4

When served cold, this becomes even more delicious and refreshing. The collagen extracted from the snow fungus also aids to thicken the soup. The almonds infuse the liquid with their unique fragrance and when poached in this lightly sweetened syrup, the pears transform from cooling and crisp to velvety and succulent. My grandma would leave a container of this in our fridge and I would stealthily slurp some up straight from the box to combat the scorching heat in the afternoons. This is also the perfect antidote for soothing a bad throat or to aid in healing coughs.

1 big snow pear
30 g dried white fungus
10 g Chinese sweet almonds
10 g Chinese bitter almonds
8 Chinese red dates
1 Tbsp Chinese wolfberries
50 g rock sugar, or to taste
1.2 litres water

1. Rinse the pear and cut into large chunks. Leave the skin on. Discard the core.
2. Soak the white fungus in water for about 20 minutes to soften. Tear the white fungus up into smaller pieces, discarding the tough inner core.
3. In a large saucepan or clay pot, add the pear, snow fungus, almonds, red dates, wolfberries, sugar and water. Let boil for about 40 minutes and leave to cool in the pot. Refrigerate overnight before serving chilled.

NOTES

- Snow fungus is known to be a beautifying food, good for the complexion and for strengthening the lungs. It has a crunchy, slippery texture and is a good sponge to sop up the flavours of whatever it has been cooked in. I've been told by the lady manning the dried goods stall in my neighbourhood market that when double-boiled, the health benefits of the snow fungus are amplified.
- Experiment with different types of pears to see which you prefer. They all poach up to different flavour profiles and textures. You could even replace the pear with papaya.

Glutinous Rice Balls

Tang Yuan

Serves 4

Every winter solstice, my grandma would cook up a batch of glutinous rice balls or *tang yuan*, little red and white dumplings in a ginger-infused broth, and send a pot of this dessert to us. I love the comforting scent of the pandan leaves and ginger as the syrup boils, alongside the slight musky scent of the glutinous rice balls. You can let the little dumplings sit around in its syrup for awhile to plump up, letting the flavours seep in even more. My grandma has been maintaining this tradition for as long as I can remember, her way of keeping the ever-expanding family in close reach. These little sticky balls of dough represent unity and familial ties, sticking to one another through thick and thin. There are many variations of these glutinous rice balls — stuffed with fragrant black sesame, coarsely ground peanuts or red bean paste — but the recipe below is based on the plain ones I grew up eating.

Glutinous Rice Dumplings
140 g glutinous rice flour
80 ml hot water
Red food colouring (optional)

Ginger Syrup
100 g mature ginger
4–5 pandan leaves
100 g rock sugar
1.2 litres water

1. Start by preparing the ginger syrup. Peel the ginger and cut into slices. Wash the pandan leaves and wipe them dry. Tie them into a knot.
2. Place the ginger, pandan leaves and rock sugar in a pot with the water. Bring to a boil, then lower the heat and let it simmer covered for about 20 minutes. Turn off the heat. If, like me, you are a ginger fiend, do this step the night before to allow the aromatics to infuse the syrup for an even more pronounced flavour. Reheat the syrup before serving.
3. Prepare the dumplings. In a bowl, mix the glutinous rice flour with the hot water until a dough forms. Set it aside to cool, then knead it until a smooth dough comes together. You may need to add more water or flour for the dough to come together. This is a pretty straightforward dough and what you're looking for is a smooth mass that's easy to work with — not too tacky or too dry.
4. If desired, apportion half the dough and add some red food colouring to tint it. Pinch bits of the dough and form into little rounds.
5. Boil a pot of water and gently lower the dumplings into the boiling water. They're done when they float. Remove them with a slotted spoon and refresh them in a pan of room temperature water to arrest the cooking process and rid them of any excess starch.
6. Place the glutinous rice balls into the ginger syrup. Spoon into bowls and enjoy!

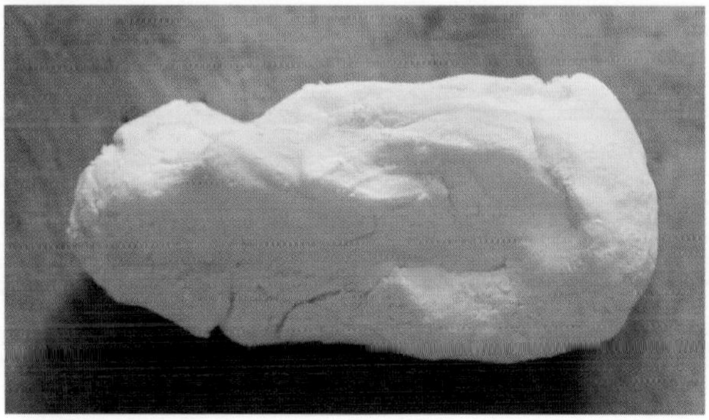

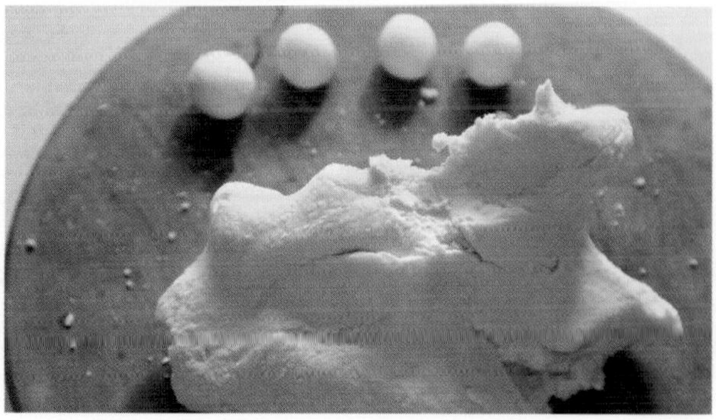

NOTES

- Using hot water to form the dough results in a chewier, springier dumpling.
- Ginger becomes more potent in flavour as it matures and the mature rhizome is typically used in braises and sweet soups. I am a ginger fiend and have a go-big-or-go-home stance with regards to any dish that has ginger as its main component, like in ginger-based soups in this instance. Depending on your proclivity, you can choose to alter the amount or type of ginger used in the recipes here.

Weights and Measures

Quantities for this book are given in Metric and American (spoon and cup) measures. Standard spoon and cup measurements used are: 1 tsp = 5 ml, 1 Tbsp = 15 ml and 1 cup = 250 ml. All measures are level unless otherwise stated.

LIQUID AND VOLUME MEASURES

Metric	**Imperial**	**American**
5 ml	1/6 fl oz	1 tsp
10 ml	1/3 fl oz	1 dessertspoon
15 ml	1/2 fl oz	1 Tbsp
60 ml	2 fl oz	1/4 cup (4 Tbsp)
85 ml	2 1/2 fl oz	1/3 cup
90 ml	3 fl oz	3/8 cup (6 Tbsp)
125 ml	4 fl oz	1/2 cup
180 ml	6 fl oz	3/4 cup
250 ml	8 fl oz	1 cup
300 ml	10 fl oz (1/2 pint)	1 1/4 cups
375 ml	12 fl oz	1 1/2 cups
435 ml	14 fl oz	1 3/4 cups
500 ml	16 fl oz	2 cups
625 ml	20 fl oz (1 pint)	2 1/2 cups
750 ml	24 fl oz (1 1/5 pints)	3 cups
1 litre	32 fl oz (1 3/5 pints)	4 cups
1.25 litres	40 fl oz (2 pints)	5 cups
1.5 litres	48 fl oz (2 2/5 pints)	6 cups
2.5 litres	80 fl oz (4 pints)	10 cups

DRY MEASURES

Metric	**Imperial**
30 grams	1 ounce
45 grams	1 1/2 ounces
55 grams	2 ounces
70 grams	2 1/2 ounces
85 grams	3 ounces
100 grams	3 1/2 ounces
110 grams	4 ounces
125 grams	4 1/2 ounces
140 grams	5 ounces
280 grams	10 ounces
450 grams	16 ounces (1 pound)
500 grams	1 pound, 1 1/2 ounces
700 grams	1 1/2 pounds
800 grams	1 3/4 pounds
1 kilogram	2 pounds, 3 ounces
1.5 kilograms	3 pounds, 4 1/2 ounces
2 kilograms	4 pounds, 6 ounces

LENGTH

Metric	**Imperial**
0.5 cm	1/4 inch
1 cm	1/2 inch
1.5 cm	3/4 inch
2.5 cm	1 inch

ABBREVIATION

tsp	teaspoon
Tbsp	tablespoon
g	gramme
kg	kilogramme
ml	millilitre